# HEARERS OF THE
# WORD

## PRAYING & EXPLORING THE READINGS
## FOR ADVENT & CHRISTMAS: YEAR A

### KIERAN J O'MAHONY OSA

Published by Messenger Publications, 2019

ISBN 978 1 78812 095 1

Designed by Messenger Publications Design Department
Cover Images: collage Shutterstock
Typeset in adobe Caslon Pro and Adobe Bitter
Printed by Hussar Books

Messenger Publications,
37 Lower Leeson Street, Dublin D02 W938
www.messenger.ie

'Beyond the Headlines'

Then I saw the wild geese flying
In fair formation to their bases in Inchicore,
And I knew that these wings would outwear the wings of war,
And a man's simple thoughts outlive the day's loud lying.
Don't fear, don't fear, I said to my soul:
The Bedlam of Time is an empty bucket rattled,
'Tis you who will say in the end who best battled.
Only they who fly home to God have flown at all.

Patrick Kavanagh, *Collected Poems*

Dedication
For Sean Goan and Jessie Rogers
Friends and colleagues in the Scripture Summer School


*'A threefold cord is not readily broken.'*
(Ecc 4:12)

# Table of Contents

Prayer before reading Holy Scripture

*Lord, inspire me to read your Scriptures and*
*to meditate upon them day and night.*
*I beg you to give me real understanding of what I read,*
*that I in turn may put its precepts into practice.*
*Yet, I know that understanding and good intentions are worthless,*
*unless rooted in your graceful love.*
*So I ask that the words of Scripture may also be not just signs on a page,*
*but channels of grace into my heart.*
*Amen.*

(Origen, AD184–253)

# Introduction

It is a particular delight to be able to offer these reflections to a wider audience. I am very grateful to Donal Neary SJ and to Messenger Publications.

As the reader will observe, these notes follow a particular sequence beginning with a first, simple reading of each passage, through somewhat detailed study, leading finally to prayer and personal reflection. It is the hope of the writer that these notes may serve two main purposes. The first goal and primary purpose is to enable people to encounter Christ through the Word of God. In other words, these notes are offered as a help to praying the Scripture and as a support for *Lectio Divina*. Accordingly, there is much emphasis on personal reflection and prayer. At the same time, the reader is invited, more or less all of the time, to hear the word not only in our contemporary context but also and perhaps first of all in the context of the time of writing. Accordingly, the notes are conceived also as a kind of ongoing course in bible study. If someone were to use the notes consistently over a period of time, the result should eventually be a solid bank of knowledge about the Scriptures – context, genre, teaching and spirituality.

The bible translation used is the New Revised Standard Version, except for the readings from Paul for which the New English Translation is used. The collects after the Gospel notes are taken with permission from Opening Prayers, a collection of collects based on the three year lectionary cycles. I could not recommend these prayers highly enough. The pointers for prayer on the Gospels are by my confrère John Byrne OSA.

Occasionally a statistic is offered in the following format: Mt (3), Mk (4), Lk (5), Jn (6), Acts (7). The numbers indicate the occurrence of a particular word in Matthew, Mark, Luke, John and Acts.

*A personal note*

When I was an undergraduate in Rome in the early 1970s, our college employed a tutor in theology, Revd Dr William (Bill) Murphy, an American priest working in the Vatican. His role was to 'locate' the theological discourse for us culturally and historically. As part of that project, we read together and explored Karl Rahner's *Hearers of the Word*. Rahner's proposal was that the human being as such is someone who listens out for a potential word from God. Even if the final personal answer is there is no God, we at least have to ask the question in response to the stirrings of the human heart. This teaching/intuition has stayed with me over all the years. Indeed, it has deepened as a result of my long engagement with Scripture. We are all 'hearers of the word' and my hope is that our listening to the Biblical word may continue to deepen and give life in abundance.

# Chapter 1

## Advent 1A

## Thought for the day

The liturgical cycle helps us not only by telling once more the story of salvation but also by underlining movements of the heart appropriate for each season. Thus, Lent invites us to conversion and Easter promotes joy in believing. What about Advent? The Advent season encourages us by taking us back to our original longing and to the original spiritual quest that brought us to God in the first place. Especially in the readings from the prophets, the lectionary explores again that restlessness of heart and helps us name our desire for the One who alone fills our hearts with his peace, 'which surpasses all understanding'.

## Prayer

*Stir up our hearts, Lord, with a great longing for you in our lives.*
*Let us feel again that deep restlessness of heart, the royal road to you.*
*Through Christ our Lord. Amen*

##  Gospel

Mt 24: 37 [Jesus said] For as the days of Noah were, so will be the coming of the Son of Man. ³⁸For as in those days before the flood they were eating and drinking, marrying and giving in marriage, until the day Noah entered the ark, ³⁹and they knew nothing until the flood came and swept them all away, so too will be the coming of the Son of Man. [40]Then two will be in the field; one will be taken and one will be left. [41]Two women will be grinding meal together; one will be taken and one will be left. [42]Keep awake therefore, for you do not know on what day your Lord is coming. [43]But understand this: if the owner of the house had known in what part of the night the thief was coming, he would have stayed awake and would not have let his house be broken into. [44]Therefore you also must be ready, for the Son of Man is coming at an unexpected hour.

## Initial observations

Advent 1 dovetails with the themes that closed the previous liturgical year, that is, the end of time, the final judgment and the appropriate preparation. Advent 2 and Advent 3 take us to two moments in the career of John the Baptist, that iconic Advent figure – his proclamation (Advent 2) and his questions about Jesus' identity (Advent 3). For Advent 4, we go backwards in time to the story of the conception of Jesus. Of course, the theme of Matthew 1:18–24 is most suitable on the Sunday nearest Christmas.

## Kind of writing

This and similar passages belong to a category of hortatory texts (*parenesis*) in the New Testament. Our reading comes from Matthew 24–25, which is that Gospel's reception of Mark 13. Matthew expands Mark and includes many parables here – parables of watchfulness. Our passage, while not exactly a parable, feels like a parable. The subsequent sequence of parables is as follows:

a) The fig tree as a parable of the coming of the Son of Man
b) As in the days of Noah
c) As when a burglar comes
d) As with a faithful servant when his master returns
e) As with bridesmaids awaiting the bridegroom
f) As with talents given to servants to work with
g) As with sheep and goats separated by the shepherd

## Old Testament background

### 'Son of Man'

The expression 'Son of Man' has two meanings. One is simply a way of referring to a human being (the usual meaning). The other is a reference to the agent of final salvation. The Book of Daniel is the source for the second understanding.

> I was watching in the night visions,
> And with the clouds of the sky
> one like a son of man was approaching.
> He went up to the Ancient of Days
> and was escorted before him.
> To him was given ruling authority, honour, and sovereignty.
> All peoples, nations, and language groups were serving him.
> His authority is eternal and will not pass away.
> His kingdom will not be destroyed. (Dn 7:13–14)

### *Noah and the Flood*

> Now the earth was corrupt in God's sight, and the earth was filled with violence. And God saw that the earth was corrupt; for all flesh had corrupted its ways upon the earth. And God said to Noah, 'I have determined to make an end of all flesh, for the earth is filled with violence because of them; now I am going to destroy them along with the earth. Make yourself an ark of cypress wood; make rooms in the ark, and cover it inside and out with pitch. This is how you are to make it: the length of the ark three hundred cubits, its width fifty cubits, and its height thirty cubits. Make a roof for the ark, and finish it to a cubit above; and put the door of the ark in its side; make it with lower, second, and third decks. For my part, I am going to bring a flood of waters on the earth, to destroy from under heaven all flesh in which is the breath of life; everything that is on the earth shall die.' (Gen 6:11–17)

## New Testament foreground

### *Themes in Matthew*

Within Matthew 24–25, similar themes arise as follows:
   a)  Watch therefore (Mt 24:42; 25:13)
   b)  Unexpected returns or arrivals (Mt 24:37, 42–44, 50; 25:10,19)
   c)  Delays in arrival (Mt 24:48; 25:5,19)
   d)  Return of the Son of Man (Mt 24:27, 30, 37, 44; 25:31)
   e)  Praises of faithful servants (Mt 24:46; 25:21, 23, 25, 34)
   f)  The use of 'Lord' (Mt 25:11, 24, 37, 44)
   g)  Exclusions from the presence (Mt 24:51; 25:10, 30, 46)

For our passage, Matthew may have in mind some of catastrophes which preceded the Jewish revolt of AD66–73, resulting in the destruction of Jerusalem.

### *The Image of the Thief*

The arresting image of the thief is likewise found across the New Testament:
   a)  For you know quite well that the day of the Lord will come in the same way as a *thief* in the night. Now when they are saying, 'There is peace and security', then sudden destruction comes on them, like labour pains on a pregnant woman, and they will surely not escape. But you, brothers and sisters, are not in the darkness for the day to overtake you like a *thief* would. For you all are sons of the light and sons of the day. We are not of the night nor of the darkness. (1 Thess 5:2–5)
   b)  But the day of the Lord will come like a *thief*; when it comes, the heavens will disappear with a horrific noise, and the celestial bodies will melt away in a blaze, and the earth and every deed done on it will be laid bare. (2 Pet 3:10)
   c)  Therefore, remember what you received and heard, and obey it, and repent. If you do not wake up, I will come like a *thief*, and you will never know at what hour I will come against you. (Rev 3:3)
   d)  Look! I will come like a *thief*! Blessed is the one who stays

alert and does not lose his clothes so that he will not have to walk around naked and his shameful condition be seen. (Rev 16:15)

## St Paul

But you, brothers and sisters, are not in the darkness for the day to overtake you like a thief would. For you all are sons of the light and sons of the day. We are not of the night nor of the darkness. So then we must not sleep as the rest, but must stay alert and sober. For those who sleep, sleep at night and those who get drunk are drunk at night. But since we are of the day, we must stay sober *by putting on the breastplate of faith* and *love* and as *a helmet our hope for salvation*. (1 Thess 5:4–8)

## Brief commentary

### (V. 37)

Something is lost by leaving out the preceding verse: 'But about that day and hour no one knows, neither the angels of heaven, nor the Son, but only the Father.' (Mt 24:36). Noah is not much mentioned in the New Testament (Mt 24:37–38; Lk 3:36; 17:26–27; Heb 11:7; 1 Pet 3:20; 2 Pet 2:5). The present mention is to illustrate unawareness, the feeling of business as usual, in the face of impending disaster. Coming is literally *parousia*, a technical used in the New Testament for the return of Jesus as the end of time. Son of Man is Jesus' self-designation and, as we saw above, it has two meanings: a human being and an agent of end-time salvation (Daniel).

### (V. 38)

The point of comparison is the lack of awareness or mindfulness of Noah's contemporaries. The Greek word for flood is the evocative *kataklysmos*. The rhythmic description conveys the soporific effect of the habitual and the usual.

(V. 39)

The people did not know. Cf. Matthew 24:36, 39, 42, 43, 44, 48, 50; 25:13. The verb to know has no object, perhaps indicating a state of general unawareness.

(V. 40)

'Taken' means to be gathered up and to enter the community of the saved at the end, just as the animals were gathered into the ark. Now invisible, the second coming will make plain who is 'in' and who is 'out'.

(V. 41)

Although the first pair of men is matched by a pair of women, Matthew is probably not thinking of gender balance. Rather, the repetition is a form of insistence or emphasis. As in the surrounding parables, the evangelist is saying that there will definitely be a time of sorting. Our choices *now*, therefore, will have an effect on our status *then*.

(V. 42)

An exhortation, drawing out the consequences of the previous teaching. Keeping awake is frequent in Mark (6) and Matthew (6). It is, understandably, absent in John and infrequent in Luke (1) and the Acts (1). By the time of Luke and Acts, the tension towards the imminent end had relaxed somewhat.

(V. 43)

A second parabolic element is introduced. Householders are not normally informed beforehand (!), another way of underlining lack of information. However there is an implied *a fortiori* argument: if a householder had this much sense to protect himself and his home, how much more the believer ought...

(V. 44)

A repetition of V. 36 forms a frame or inclusion. The theme of being ready is a feature of these parables in Matthew: Matthew 22:4, 8; 24:44; 25:10. Unexpected renders a blunter, more direct expression in Greek: in the hour *you do not know*, the Son of Man is coming.

## Pointers for prayer

a) The 'coming of the Son of Man' can be applied to the end of the world, to the moment of death, or indeed to any moment of grace. We are not given advance notice as to when any of these will happen, so the message is to be alert and ready. When have you found that your alertness meant that you were able to receive an unexpected grace (e.g. take an opportunity which presented itself, or respond to a hint from another person that you might easily have missed, etc.).

b) One of the enemies of alert living is constant busyness. Have you ever found that being caught up in your own agenda makes you less sensitive to what is happening around you? Recall times when you paused in your relentless busyness and were rewarded by a significant interchange with another person, a moment of grace.

c) You probably know the difference between being ready for a visitor and the unannounced caller who catches you unprepared. Let the memory of the discomfort of being caught off guard spur you on to a constant readiness for the coming of the Lord.

## Prayer

*God of majesty and power, amid the clamour of our violence*
*your Word of truth resounds; upon a world made dark by sin*
*the Sun of Justice casts his dawning rays.*

*Keep your household watchful and aware of the hour in which we live.*

*Hasten the advent of that day when the sounds of war will be for ever*
*stilled, the darkness of evil scattered, and all your children gathered into one.*

*We ask this through him whose coming is certain, whose day draws near:*
*your Son, our Lord Jesus Christ, who lives and reigns with you in the*
*unity of the Holy Spirit, God for ever and ever. Amen.*

## 🌿 Second Reading 🌿

**Rom 13:11** And do this because we know the time, that it is already the hour for us to awake from sleep, for our salvation is now nearer than when we became believers. [12]The night has advanced toward dawn; the day is near. So then we must lay aside the works of darkness, and put on the weapons of light. [13]Let us live decently as in the daytime, not in carousing and drunkenness, not in sexual immorality and sensuality, not in discord and jealousy. [14]Instead, put on the Lord Jesus Christ, and make no provision for the flesh to arouse its desires.

## Initial observations

Three times Advent year A we hear from the letter to the Romans. Today's excerpt is apocalyptic in tone and takes up the contrasting themes of light and darkness, vigilance and sleep.

## Kind of writing

The final chapters of Romans are exhortations, in the genre of deliberative rhetoric. In the chart below, the different moments are identified. The lectionary excerpt is an integral unit from chapter 13. In effect, it constitutes a mini–conclusion, a more emotional exhortation in apocalyptic mode at the end of the foregoing instructions in Romans 12:3–13:10.

a)  Christian life as 'reasonable worship' (Rom 12:1–2)
b)  What does Christian living require? (Rom 12:3–13:14)
  •  Your own gifts (Rom 12:3–8)
  •  Gift of love within the community (Rom 12:9–16)
  •  Love in action outside the community (Rom 12:17–21)
  •  How should we treat civil authorities? (Rom 13:1–7)
  •  Being indebted in love (Rom 13:8–10)
  •  'Knowing the time' (Rom 13:11–14)
c)  Living 'inclusively' and in tolerance of each other (Rom 14:1–15:6)

- Tolerance is the call of everyone (Rom 14:1–12)
- Especially the strong should be tolerant of the weak (Rom 14:13–23)
- The example of Jesus, who was himself so patient (Rom 15:1–6)

## Context in the community

The letter to the Romans was written to house churches in Rome which were divided along Gentile/Jewish lines. Most of the letter is given over to the great theological arguments of Romans 1–11. Paul shows again and again that God makes no distinction between Jews and Gentiles whether in terms of sin or grace.

The practical consequences for both Jews and Gentiles of Paul's 'reading' of the Christ event are then offered in Romans 12:1–15:6. These are very fruitful, deeply pastoral chapters, perhaps unjustly overshadowed by the preceding mighty arguments. And yet, the whole theological sweep of Romans is rendered practical in these final chapters: here is the goal of the whole project. The overall message at this point is the practice of love and the living of tolerance.

## Related passages

Now on the topic of times and seasons, brothers and sisters, you have no need for anything to be written to you. For you know quite well that the day of the Lord will come in the same way as a thief in the night. Now when they are saying, 'There is peace and security', then sudden destruction comes on them, like labor pains on a pregnant woman, and they will surely not escape. But you, brothers and sisters, are not in the darkness for the day to overtake you like a thief would. For you all are sons of the light and sons of the day. We are not of the night nor of the darkness. So then we must not sleep as the rest, but must stay alert and sober. For those who sleep, sleep at night and those who get drunk are drunk at night. But since we are of the day, we must stay sober by putting on the breastplate of faith and love and as a helmet our hope for salvation. For God did not destine us for wrath but for gaining salvation through our Lord Jesus Christ. He died for us so that whether we are alert or asleep we will come to life together with him. Therefore encourage one another and build up each other, just as you are in fact doing. (1 Thess 5:1–11)

## Brief commentary

The vocabulary used is taken from Apocalyptic: time, hour, sleep, night, day, darkness, weapons, daytime, put on. Cf. 1 Thessalonians 5:1–11 above.

(V. 11)
We start with the Pauline theme of the already and not yet. Cf. Mark 14:41. 'For everything made evident is light, and for this reason it says: "Awake, O sleeper! Rise from the dead, and Christ will shine on you!"' (Eph 5:14)

(V. 12)
The times demand behaviour consistent with our convictions. The adjective 'nearer' from V. 11 becomes a verb here. The same verb is used by Jesus for his proclamation of the kingdom: 'The time is fulfilled, and the kingdom of God has come near' (Mk 1:15). The imagery of weapons of defence fits the context of the final apocalyptic showdown.

(V. 13)
'Let us live' is literally 'let us walk around',, using the usual Rabbinic image of walking for moral behaviour. 'Decently' as an adverb is a Pauline usage (Rom 13:13; 1 Cor 14:40; 1 Thess 4:12) in the New Testament. The general meaning of noble or eminent is narrowed to mean conduct which is respectable to outsiders. In that context of outsiders, cf. '… but all things should be done decently and in order' (1 Cor 14:40). To the usual marks of nightlife excess, Paul pointedly adds discord and jealousy, the besetting sin which triggered the letter. Placing them on the same level is a sharp critique of the Christ-believers of both backgrounds in the Roman house churches.

(V. 14)

The important verb 'to put on' is resumed more explicitly. Cf. 'But since we are of the day, we must stay sober by putting on the breastplate of faith and love and as a helmet our hope for salvation' (1 Thess 5:8). Thus values of the world are set aside in favour of the upside-down values of the kingdom.

## Pointers for prayer

a) A wake-up call is almost always timely. Is there something in me or in my life in need of a fresh beginning?

b) Putting on the Lord Jesus: what am I doing concretely to enable such a deep and personal transformation?

## Prayer

*Help us, life-affirming God, to put on Christ and so bear witness to you by how we live. Help us to let go of whatever stands in the way of our continued conversion to Christ, who lives and reigns with you in the unity of the Holy Spirit, God for ever and ever. Amen.*

## 🌿 First Reading 🌿

Isa 2:1 Here is the message about Judah and Jerusalem
that was revealed to Isaiah son of Amoz.

2 In the future
the mountain of the LORD's temple will endure
as the most important of mountains,
and will be the most prominent of hills.
All the nations will stream to it,

3 many peoples will come and say,
'Come, let us go up to the LORD's mountain,
to the temple of the God of Jacob,
so he can teach us his requirements,
and we can follow his standards.'

> For Zion will be the centre for moral instruction;
> the LORD will issue edicts from Jerusalem.
>
> 4    He will judge disputes between nations;
> he will settle cases for many peoples.
> They will beat their swords into ploughshares,
> and their spears into pruning hooks.
> Nations will not take up the sword against
> other nations,
> and they will no longer train for war.
>
> 5    O descendants of Jacob,
> come, let us walk in the LORD's guiding light.

## Initial observations

The liturgical year starts today and, very appropriately, it begins with an invitation. The pilgrim people hears a renewed call to undertake the journey of faith, not to a particular promontory, but to God himself, our rock, that he may teach us his ways.

## Kind of writing

The writing is in the style typical biblical poetry. However, the parts are distinct. The usual parallelism – a technique of saying the same thing twice – is especially clear in 2bc, 3bc, 3de, 3fg, 4ab, 4cd, 4ef. It gives great energy to the message.

*Structure of Isaiah 2:1–22*

a) (V. 1) A superscription
b) (Vs 2–4) An oracle for Jerusalem
c) (Vs 5–22) An oracle against Jacob

## Origin of the reading

The book of Isaiah as it now stands is a result of a long, yet unified evolution. The unifying thread is threefold: national sin, disaster (read as punishment) and restoration (salvation). The agents of punishments noted in Isaiah are the Assyria, Babylon and Persia. There is no attempt, by the final editors, to airbrush out the parts that belong to specific periods, such as our reading today. The book divides into three grand portions: Isaiah 1–39, 40–55, 55–66. However, within the large sections are texts from different contexts.

In Isaiah 1–39, the presenting issues are social injustice and false worship. Our excerpt opens a section taking in Isaiah 2–4 or possibly Isaiah 2–12. The opening line marks a fresh start.

## Related passages

> Great is the LORD and greatly to be praised in the city of our God. His holy mountain, beautiful in elevation, is the joy of all the earth, Mount Zion, in the far north, the city of the great King. (Ps 48:1–2)

An almost identical reprise is found in Micah 4:1–3.

## Brief commentary

(V. 1)
The title is in contrast with an earlier title: 'Therefore, the sovereign LORD who commands armies, the powerful ruler of Israel, says this: "Ah, I will seek vengeance against my adversaries, I will take revenge against my enemies."' (Isa 1:24) It may be that the ascription of the 'word' to Isaiah son of Amoz in a counter blast to Micah's use of the oracle which follows (see above). Although the time frame seems the same as in Isaiah 1:1, in V. 2, we are told this oracle was after these days.

(V. 2)
The theme of the mountain of the Lord is typical of Isaiah 1–37 and conversely absent in Isaiah 38–55. Zion is to become the pilgrimage city not just for Israelites but for all the nations. Cf. 'I will bring them to my holy mountain; I will make them happy in the temple where people pray to me. Their burnt offerings and sacrifices will be accepted on my altar, for my temple will be known as a temple where all nations may

pray. The sovereign LORD says this, the one who gathers the dispersed of Israel: I will still gather them up' (Isa 56:7–8). Streaming is unique here to Isaiah (and Micah): it reverses nature because this flow is uphill!

(V. 3)

The significance of the temple is not sacrifice but instruction (*torah*). Here the people are gathered to learn the ways of the Lord. The parallelism is itself instructive: not only to the mountain but *also to the house*; not only to be taught *but also to walk*; not only for *Torah* but also for *the Word of the Lord*. What is at stake is dynamic learning, so that we live what we have heard. It its final editing, in the time of Ezra and Nehemiah, 'torah' meant both instruction for the social order internationally and the teaching of the five books of Moses.

(V. 4)

This tremendous vision informs all of Isaiah and is fully developed in Isaiah 41. YHWH will be sovereign over all peoples and war will no longer be necessary. Against the narrow nationalism of Ezra and Nehemiah, here it God, not one nation which rules. The unlearning of war puts words on a perennial human desire.

(V. 5)

This verse, beginning with a different address and a different subject, really open a distinct oracle which takes in Vs 5–22. This verse introduces a theme which will turn through all of Isaiah: the contrast between light and darkness. Contrast: 'Therefore justice is far from us, and righteousness does not reach us; we wait for light, and lo! there is darkness; and for brightness, but we walk in gloom. We grope like the blind along a wall, groping like those who have no eyes; we stumble at noon as in the twilight, among the vigorous as though we were dead.' (Isa 59:9–10)

## Pointers for prayer

a) At the start of the liturgical year, the reading surely touches a chord in each of us to take up again with renewed vigour the pilgrimage of faith.

b) The transformation in the reading is interior: and they will no longer *train* for war. In ways less dramatic but no less real, we all need to go within and look at our inner motivations and convictions. Conversion is never done and dusted!

## Prayer

*God, loving and insistent, let us hear again your voice within.*
*It is your word which guides us and we pray that,*
*in this season of Advent, your word may penetrate our hearts*
*and continue to change our lives. Through Christ our Lord. Amen.*

# Chapter 2

## Advent 2A

## Thought for the day

It is possible to live a merely sentient existence, paying attention only to the immediate and being satisfied once the urgent, obvious appetites are met. It is hard to say how many manage to sustain this form of sleepwalking! In our better moments, we all know that this is wholly inadequate, even on a merely human level. We are all of us called to rise above above mere existence and to live life abundantly (cf. Jn 10:10). In the faith, the Advent call is to wake up from our slumbers. *Metanoia* (conversion or repentance) means a whole change of mindset, going right down to the roots of our being. It's the only game in town. Of course it takes time, but the time is *now*.

## Prayer

*God of life abundant, may your advent call to life and love,*
*hope and conversion touch us again and draw us closer to you. Amen.*

## 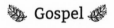 Gospel

**Mt 3:1** In those days John the Baptist appeared in the wilderness of Judea, proclaiming, ²'Repent, for the kingdom of heaven has come near'. ³This is the one of whom the prophet Isaiah spoke when he said, 'The voice of one crying out in the wilderness: "Prepare the way of the Lord, make his paths straight"'.

⁴Now John wore clothing of camel's hair with a leather belt around his waist, and his food was locusts and wild honey. ⁵Then the people of Jerusalem and all Judea were going out to him, and all the region along the Jordan, ⁶and they were baptised by him in the river Jordan, confessing their sins.

⁷But when he saw many Pharisees and Sadducees coming for baptism, he said to them, 'You brood of vipers! Who warned you to flee from the wrath to come? ⁸Bear fruit worthy of repentance. ⁹Do not presume to say to yourselves, 'We have Abraham as our ancestor'; for I tell you, God is able from these stones to raise up children to Abraham. ¹⁰Even now the ax is lying at the root of the trees; every tree therefore that does not bear good fruit is cut down and thrown into the fire.

¹¹'I baptise you with water for repentance, but one who is more powerful than I is coming after me; I am not worthy to carry his sandals. He will baptise you with the Holy Spirit and fire. ¹²His winnowing fork is in his hand, and he will clear his threshing floor and will gather his wheat into the granary; but the chaff he will burn with unquenchable fire.'

## Initial observations

Advent 2 introduces the seasonal figure of John the Baptist, the prophet who ushered in the ministry of Jesus himself. Jesus was a disciple of John and began his public ministry only when his mentor was arrested and could no longer function. Jesus' proclamation resembles that of John – repentance/conversion – but the dreadful events predicted by John are replaced by Jesus' message of God's mercy and compassion.

## Kind of writing

The first part of the text, presenting the person, proclamation, figure and baptism of John, is a *chreia*, a short story which illustrates the essentials of John. The second part of the text elaborates the preaching in the direction of practical exhortation. The last part reflects John's suspicion that he was preparing for a greater figure – even though the actual ministry of Jesus came not with ferocity but with forgiveness.

## Old Testament background

### Isaiah and Malachi

The citation from Isaiah is subtly adjusted to make it 'fit ' John as a figure in the wilderness. Hence it is taken to read: a voice cries out in the wilderness, 'prepare etc.'. There is, of course, no point in crying out in the wilderness – nobody lives there.

A voice cries out, 'In the wilderness clear a way for the LORD; construct in the desert a road for our God.' (Isa 40:3).

The other quotation from Malachi 3:1 (mistakenly attributed to Isaiah in Mark 1:2–3) is located elsewhere by Matthew, a bit of a scholar or a pedant, depending on your point of view! 'This is the one about whom it is written, "See, I am sending my messenger ahead of you, who will prepare your way before you"' (Mt 11:10).

### John as Elijah and Samson

John the Baptist is presented with traits of Elijah and Samson, prophetic figures: 'they replied, "He was a hairy man and had a leather belt tied around his waist". The king said, "He is Elijah the Tishbite"'.(2 Kings 1:8).

> Some time later, when Samson went back to marry her, he turned aside to see the lion's remains. He saw a swarm of bees in the lion's carcass, as well as some honey. He scooped it up with his hands and ate it as he walked along. When he returned to his father and mother, he offered them some and they ate it. But he did not tell them he had scooped the honey out of the lion's carcass. (Judg 14:8–9)

## New Testament foreground

*John in the Gospels*

John the Baptist is a very important figure in the history of Jesus. All four Gospels include him but in quite different ways. For instance, only Luke has the story of his birth. According to Matthew, John is the expected Elijah; according to the Fourth Gospel, he himself says he is not! Mark reports the baptism without any apparent unease. Matthew is uneasy; Luke, narratively speaking, has John is prison for the baptism; John omits the baptism altogether, although the related phenomena are recounted. John definitely baptised Jesus – the discomfort with it proves it took place and was not invented. Again only two Gospels report his death, lest any comparison with the death of Jesus be encouraged.

*Similarities with Jesus*

Like John, Jesus withdrew to the desert – an implied critique of the Jerusalem temple cult, like the people in Qumran. Like John, Jesus expected the kingdom and proclaimed repentance/conversion marked through an immersion ritual.

*John on Jesus*

We may say that John was right and wrong about Jesus. He expected tremendous judgment but Jesus came in mercy and compassion. John did send to enquire about Jesus, but we are not told what his reaction to the information was.

> Then the disciples of John came to him, saying, 'Why do we and the Pharisees fast often, but your disciples do not fast?' And Jesus said to them, 'The wedding guests cannot mourn as long as the bridegroom is with them, can they? The days will come when the bridegroom is taken away from them, and then they will fast. No one sews a piece of unshrunk cloth on an old cloak, for the patch pulls away from the cloak, and a worse tear is made. Neither is new wine put into old wineskins; otherwise, the skins burst, and the wine is spilled, and the skins are destroyed; but new wine is put into fresh wineskins, and so both are preserved.' (Mt 9:14–17)

When John heard in prison what the Messiah was doing, he sent word by his disciples and said to him, 'Are you the one who is to come, or are we to wait for another?' Jesus answered them, 'Go and tell John what you hear and see: the blind receive their sight, the lame walk, the lepers are cleansed, the deaf hear, the dead are raised, and the poor have good news brought to them. And blessed is anyone who takes no offence at me.' (Mt 11:2–6)

## St Paul

For even if I made you sad by my letter, I do not regret having written it (even though I did regret it, for I see that my letter made you sad, though only for a short time). Now I rejoice, not because you were made sad, but because you were made sad to the point of repentance. For you were made sad as God intended, so that you were not harmed in any way by us. For sadness as intended by God produces a repentance that leads to salvation, leaving no regret, but worldly sadness brings about death. For see what this very thing, this sadness as God intended, has produced in you: what eagerness, what defence of yourselves, what indignation, what alarm, what longing, what deep concern, what punishment! In everything you have proved yourselves to be innocent in this matter. (2 Cor 7:8–11)

## Brief commentary

(V. 1)
Wilderness is the place of encounter, return and prophecy. It was also the place to which people like John withdrew in some disgust at the religious leadership which they regarded as having become polluted.

(V. 2)
Repent really means convert, a whole journey and change of mindset. Kingdom of God is a kind of 'code' for God's future intervention,

establishing lasting justice, in the face of evident injustice and tragedy.

(V. 3)

In this verse, John is associated with the return from the Babylonian Exile. Punctuation matters. The Isaiah quotation, as we saw above, is adjusted so that the voice cries out in the wilderness, to match the ministry of John in the desert.

(V. 4)

The details indicate he is the expected Elijah. Cf. 2 Kings 1:8 above.

(Vs 5–6)

The popular reaction to John is evident also in the need to have him executed. The mention of the Jordan reminds us of Joshua, who brought people across the river to the Promised Land. The location is a powerful illustration of the purpose of John the Baptist.

(V. 7)

It is hard to imagine the Sadducees (temple conservatives) coming to John, but some must have been touched by his message. Still, the prophet did not ingratiate himself! This preaching is very like the preaching of Jesus in Matthew, where we read:

> Either make the tree good, and its fruit good; or make the tree bad, and its fruit bad; for the tree is known by its fruit. You brood of vipers! How can you speak good things, when you are evil? For out of the abundance of the heart the mouth speaks. The good person brings good things out of a good treasure, and the evil person brings evil things out of an evil treasure. I tell you, on the day of judgment you will have to give an account for every careless word you utter; for by your words you will be justified, and by your words you will be condemned. (Mt 12:33–37)

Relying on status or tradition, however holy, is robustly, not to say violently, set aside by John.

(V. 11)

Carrying sandals was the role of the lowest slave. It is possible that, historically, John spoke of wind (*pneuma*) and fire, elevated theologically to the Holy Spirit (*pneuma*) / and fire by the tradition or the gospel writer. Thus three of the classical elements were brought into play by John: air, fire and water. The later Christian reception of his teaching identified the wind of judgment with the Holy Spirit.

(V. 12)
Severe judgment is his clear expectation. Harvest imagery is often used in the Bible to indicate the time of sorting after the harvest. For example: 'The wicked are not so, but are like chaff that the wind drives away' (Ps 1:4).

## Pointers for prayer

a)  John the Baptist came to bear witness to Jesus. Who have been the people who have borne witness to us of the good news of the gospel that God loves us – a friend, a parent, a teacher, etc.? To whom have we borne that witness?

b)  John appears in the story as one who had the courage to be himself in the face of opposition. He was also a person who knew his own value, did not make exaggerated claims and was content with his mission. Can you recall times when you have been content to be yourself, without pretending to be more than you are? What was it like to have that freedom, even in the face of criticism from others?

c)  John was 'the voice of one crying out in the wilderness' – announcing confidently to those in the wilderness that they must not despair because God's grace may come to them at any moment.

d)  Have you had the experience of being in the wilderness, feeling lost? From whom did you hear a voice that gave you hope? Have you been able to give hope to other people when they were in the wilderness?

# Prayer

*Your kingdom is at hand, O God of justice and peace;*
*you made John the Baptist its herald to announce the coming of your Christ,*
*who baptises with the Holy Spirit and with fire.*

*Give us a spirit of repentance to make us worthy of the kingdom.*
*Let complacency yield to conviction, that in our day justice will flourish*
*and conflict give way to the peace you bestow in Christ.*

*We ask this through him whose coming is certain, whose day draws near:*
*your Son, our Lord Jesus Christ, who lives and reigns with you*
*in the unity of the Holy Spirit, God for ever and ever. Amen.*

## 🌿 Second Reading 🌿

**Rom 15:** *¹But we who are strong ought to bear with the failings of the weak, and not just please ourselves. ²Let each of us please his neighbour for his good to build him up. ³For even Christ did not please himself, but just as it is written, 'The insults of those who insult you have fallen on me'.* ⁴For everything that was written in former times was written for our instruction, so that through endurance and through encouragement of the scriptures we may have hope. ⁵Now may the God of endurance and comfort give you unity with one another in accordance with Christ Jesus, ⁶so that together you may with one voice glorify the God and Father of our Lord Jesus Christ.

⁷Receive one another, then, just as Christ also received you, to God's glory. ⁸For I tell you that Christ has become a servant of the circumcised on behalf of God's truth to confirm the promises made to the fathers, ⁹and thus the Gentiles glorify God for his mercy. As it is written, 'Because of this I will confess you among the Gentiles, and I will sing praises to your name.'

## Initial observations

Significant Christian vocabulary makes this reading especially suitable for Advent: endurance, hope, mercy. We may add the role of Scripture in our lives.

## Kind of writing

The excerpt chosen in the lectionary offers us the final verses of the Fourth Proof and the opening verses of the Conclusion or *peroratio*. This should be clear from a glance at the outline. In Vs 4–6, Paul is drawing a longer argument to a conclusion while in Vs 7–9 he is commencing the summing up of the whole of Romans.

*Fourth Proof*

Romans 12:1–15:6: Practical advice on living tolerantly.

Living 'inclusively' and in tolerance of each other (Rom 14:1–15:6):
  a) Tolerance is the call of everyone (Rom 14:1–12).
  b) Especially the strong should be tolerant of the weak (Rom 14:13–23).
  c) The example of Jesus, who was so patient (Rom 15:1–6).

*Conclusion*
  a) Summary (Rom 15:7–13)
  b) Reasons for coming to Rome (Rom 15:14–29)
  c) Final appeal (Rom 15:30–33)

## Context in the community

The Roman house churches were divided regarding how much of the Jewish tradition should be retained and practiced: circumcision, dietary laws and Sabbath observance. It mattered to Paul because the new fellowship of Jew and Gentile stood at the centre of his Gospel. He wrote the longest of his letters hoping to help the Christians in Rome to live together richly and tolerantly.

## Related passages

As usual in Paul, the thesis of whole letter is programmatic. Below you find inserted into the thesis the major sections where the various topics are taken up.

> Rom 1:16 For I am not ashamed of the gospel, for it is God's power for salvation [corresponding to Romans 5–8] to everyone who believes [corresponding to Romans 1–4], to the Jew first and also to the Greek [corresponding to Romans 9–11]. [17]For the righteousness of God is revealed in the gospel from faith to faith, just as it is written, 'The righteous by faith will live' [corresponding to Romans 12–15].

## Brief commentary

### (V. 4)

Paul has just cited scripture in V. 3 (and indeed throughout the letter). The key words are part of the apocalyptic and preaching vocabulary of early Christianity: teaching (*didaskalia*), endurance (*hupomonē*), encouragement (*paraklēsis*), hope (*elpis*).

### (V. 5a)

The prayer flows naturally from the previous verse repeating two key words. The Greek word *paraklēsis* means both comfort and encouragement.

### (Vs 5b–6)

Paul concludes the Fourth Proof with this fitting prayer, addressing directly the issue of the sharp divisions in the Roman house churches, praying for oneness of heart and mind.

### (V. 7)

This is really the heart of Romans 12–15. The plain and direct exhortation has a massive background across the whole letter, thus underling the function of summary: *receive* (Rom 14:1, 3) *one another* (Rom 1:12, 27; 2:15; 12:5, 10, 16; 13:8; 14:13, 19; 15:5), *then, just as*

*Christ also received you, to God's glory* (Rom 1:23; 2:7, 10; 3:7, 23; 4:20; 5:2; 6:4; 8:18, 21; 9:4, 23; 11:36).'

(V. 8)

V. 8 corresponds to Romans 1–4, 9–11. The grand story of salvation, its origins in Judaism and the extension of grace of all without distinction is summarised. V. 8 discretely gathers in much of the wording and teaching of the letter: '*for I tell you that Christ has become* (Rom 1:3, 2:25; 3:19; 4:18; 6:2, 15, 20; 7:3–4; 9:29; 10:20; 11:5–6, 9, 17, 25, 34; 12:16) *a servant* (Rom 13:4) *of the circumcised* (Rom 2:25–3:1; 3:30; 4:9–12) *on behalf of God's truth* (Rom 1:18, 25; 2:2, 8, 20; 3:7; 9:1) *to confirm the promises* (Rom 4:13–14, 16, 20; 9:4, 8–9) *made to the fathers* (Rom 4:11–12, 16–18; 9:5, 10; 11:28).'

(V. 9)

V. 9 corresponds to Romans 5–8. The mercy and salvation of God are fully explored in the Second Proof, Romans 5–8. 9b begins a mighty series of biblical citations, confirming the teaching in V. 4. Again, this verse has a background in the letter: '*And thus the Gentiles* (Rom 1:5, 13; 2:14, 24; 3:29; 4:17–18; 9:24, 30; 10:19; 11:11–13, 25) *glorify* (Rom 1:21; 8:30; 11:13; 15:6) *God for his mercy* (Rom 9:23; 11:21).'

## Pointers for prayer

a) In your experience, has Scripture brought you endurance, encouragement and hope?

b) We are to welcome one another just as Christ has welcomed us. This is not always easy. Where does the challenge lie for you?

c) We regularly call down the mercy (*eleos*) of God: '*Kyrie eleison*'. In words beloved of St Teresa of Ávila: 'the mercies of the Lord I will sing for ever'.

## Prayer

*By your grace, loving God, we have the gift of the Scriptures. With the continued help your grace,*

*may listen deeply to what you want to say to each one.*
*May we know your gifts of endurance, encouragement and hope,*
*so that not only our lips but also our lives*
*may be a song in praise of your mercy. Through Christ our Lord. Amen.*

## 🌿 First Reading 🌿

*Chorus*

**Isa 11:1** A shoot will grow out of Jesse's root stock,
a bud will sprout from his roots.

² The Lord's spirit will rest on him—
a spirit that gives extraordinary wisdom,
a spirit that provides the ability to execute plans,
a spirit that produces absolute loyalty to the Lord.

³ He will take delight in obeying the Lord.

*Comment*

He will not judge by mere appearances,
or make decisions on the basis of hearsay.

⁴ He will treat the poor fairly,
and make right decisions for the downtrodden
of the earth.
He will strike the earth with the rod of his mouth,
and order the wicked to be executed.

*Chorus*

⁵ Justice will be like a belt around his waist,
integrity will be like a belt around his hips.

⁶ A wolf will reside with a lamb,
and a leopard will lie down with a young goat;
an ox and a young lion will graze together,

as a small child leads them along.
7   A cow and a bear will graze together,
their young will lie down together.
A lion, like an ox, will eat straw.
8   A baby will play
over the hole of a snake;
over the nest of a serpent
an infant will put his hand.

*YHWH*

9   They will no longer injure or destroy
on my entire royal mountain.
For there will be universal submission to the
LORD's sovereignty,
just as the waters completely cover the sea.

*Monarchist*

[10]At that time a root from Jesse will stand like a signal flag for the nations. Nations will look to him for guidance, and his residence will be majestic. [11]At that time the sovereign master will again lift his hand to reclaim the remnant of his people from Assyria, Egypt, Pathros, Cush, Elam, Shinar, Hamath, and the seacoasts.

## Initial observations

This is a (perhaps *the*) typical Isaiah reading for Advent. It voices a longing for salvation and a confidence that God will be faithful to ancient divine promises. The third part is glorious but difficult in the real world. People may well wonder why it is being read. The claims, descriptions and metaphors 'pirouette' in a bewildering dance!

## Kind of writing

This is a kind of dramatised dialogue and to make the steps clear, 'voices' have been added to the text in italics to signal the changes of speakers.

The usual parallelism is quite evident and the reading is framed by reference to Jesse, the father of David (stump, branch and root). See the related passages further down.

## Origin of the reading

Our reading comes from First Isaiah, i.e. Isaiah 1–39 from chapters 1–12. The full layout is here:

1–12: Condemnation and salvation; Davidic king; Assyria as God's instrument
13–23: Oracles concerning foreign nations
24–27: Judgment on the whole world
28–33: Judah confronts Assyria and Egypt
34–35: Salvation comes to Judah
36–39: Historical notes on Isaiah, Hezekiah and Jerusalem

## Related passages

Now these are the descendants of Perez: Perez became the father of Hezron, Hezron of Ram, Ram of Amminadab, Amminadab of Nahshon, Nahshon of Salmon, Salmon of Boaz, Boaz of Obed, Obed of Jesse, and Jesse of David. (Ruth 4:18–22)

## Brief commentary

(Vs 2–3a)
These verses describe God's gifts to this future king. There is a strong feeling of wisdom (sapiential) qualities here, perhaps echoing the first descendant of David, Solomon, famous for his proverbs.

(Vs 3b–5)
It is not quite clear who is the subject of the affirmations here, but mostly likely it is the future anointed king. The qualities are traditional: impartial justice, effective speech, faithfulness. From a literary point of view, notice the body language: eyes, ear, mouth, lips, waist and loins.

(Vs 6–8)

This pastoral idyll of nature reconciled has a basis in actual practice. It was the custom to have a young boy (or even a girl) act as village herder to lead out the domestic animals – sheep, goats and calves – to pasture in the morning and to bring them back in evening to enjoy what shade they might find. The addition of dangerous wild life is acknowledged in an earlier David story in 1 Samuel 17:34–37. The evocation of this Davidic episode is no doubt intentional.

(V. 9)

Zion as the holy mountain is a regular feature in David traditions. It is expanded here to include the whole earth as under the rule of YHWH.

(V. 10)

The commentator affirms a future restoration of the Davidic monarchy, which will be unlike the disastrous rule of the divided monarchy. That monarchy emphatically did not represent God on earth, in justice and equity. The renewed monarchy will become the envy of other nations and people will come to Zion seeking wisdom, just as the queen of Sheba made her way to Solomon.

## Pointers for prayer

a) Go back in your own experiences and recall when you needed the gifts of wisdom, courage and 'fear of the Lord'. What was it like for you? Do you need these gifts today?

b) The idyllic scene of nature in harmony and antagonisms reconciled puts it up to us. Where in my life to I need reconciliation? Is there any 'unfinished business' in important relationships?

## Prayer

*Loving God, you hold out to us the hope of reconciliation and new life.*
*In this time of Advent, open our hearts to receive your gifts of*
*wisdom and courage and so lead us more deeply into your own life.*
*Through Christ our Lord. Amen.*

# Chapter 3

## Advent 3A

## Thought for the day

Joy in believing might seem an 'extra' in today's challenging climate for faith. Many of us struggle simply to hold on to faith, not to mention being exuberant about it all. And yet, of course there is deep happiness in faith. First of all, everything around us is a gift and behind all the gifts stands the giver. Secondly, love is at the heart of it all and, in the faith, nothing is ever 'lost' or 'wasted'. Faith, hope and love endure and the greatest of these is love. Finally, why not 'permit' ourselves true joy in all that God has done for us and still does for us in Jesus and in the Holy Spirit?

## Prayer

*We believe, loving God, that you take delight in all you have made.*
*Open up in us again the springs of joy, that we may delight in you,*
*our true joy. Through Christ our Lord. Amen.*

## 🌿 Gospel 🌿

**Mt 11:2** When John heard in prison what the Messiah was doing, he sent word by his disciples ³and said to him, 'Are you the one who is to come, or are we to wait for another?' ⁴Jesus answered them, 'Go and tell John what you hear and see: ⁵the blind receive their sight, the lame walk, the lepers are cleansed, the deaf hear, the dead are raised, and the poor have good news brought to them. [6]And blessed is anyone who takes no offence at me.'

[7]As they went away, Jesus began to speak to the crowds about John: 'What did you go out into the wilderness to look at? A reed shaken by the wind? [8]What then did you go out to see? Someone dressed in soft robes? Look, those who wear soft robes are in royal palaces. [9]What then did you go out to see? A prophet? Yes, I tell you, and more than a prophet. [10]This is the one about whom it is written,

"See, I am sending my messenger ahead of you, who will prepare your way before you."

[11]Truly I tell you, among those born of women no one has arisen greater than John the Baptist; yet the least in the kingdom of heaven is greater than he.'

## Initial observations

John the Baptist asks the question we all ask: is *this* the one? The question may seem a strange one given that (a) in Luke 1–2 they are supposed to have been cousins and (b) Jesus had been a disciple of John. As for (a), it would seem clear that the family link is a later metaphor for their theological relatedness. As for (b), we really know very little of their actual relationship. Jesus was indeed a disciple of John. John did baptise Jesus. Jesus started his ministry once John was arrested, apparently. It would seem that Jesus saw John as an authentic and important prophet (cf. Mt 11:7–15; 21:23–27).

Furthermore, only when John could no longer function did Jesus enter the public arena. How much they knew each other personally remains unanswerable for lack of evidence.

## Kind of writing

There are two anecdotes here, each with a slightly extraneous punch line. The second story (about the identity of John) depends on the first (about the identity of Jesus).

## Old Testament background

### *The Language of Isaiah*

The response of Jesus is in the language of Isaiah: 'Then blind eyes will open, deaf ears will hear. Then the lame will leap like a deer, the mute tongue will shout for joy;for water will flow in the desert, streams in the wilderness' (Isa 35:5–6).

> The spirit of the sovereign LORD is upon me, because the LORD has chosen me. He has commissioned me to encourage the poor, to help the brokenhearted, to decree the release of captives, and the freeing of prisoners, to announce the year when the LORD will show his favour, the day when our God will seek vengeance, to console all who mourn, to strengthen those who mourn in Zion, by giving them a turban, instead of ashes, oil symbolising joy, instead of mourning, a garment symbolising praise, instead of discouragement. They will be called oaks of righteousness, trees planted by the LORD to reveal his splendour. (Isa 61:1–3)

See also Isaiah 26:19; 29:18; 42:7, 18.

## New Testament foreground

### *John in Mathew*

John the Baptist is mentioned in Matthew very frequently: preaching (Mt 3:1–12), baptism (Mt 3:13–17), arrest (Mt 4:12), enquiry (Mt 11:2–6), as Elijah (Mt 11:7–15), comparison with Jesus (Mt 11:16–19), death (Mt 14:1–12) and authority (Mt 21:23–27). Quite a large presence.

### 'The One Who Is to Come'

'The one who is to come' is a phrase regularly found of the Messiah in Matthew (Mt 3:11; 11:3; 16:28; 21:9; 23:39; 24:30; 26:64). As such, the expectation remains unclear.

### Disciples of John

Matthew 11:2; 14:12, Mark, Q and John agree in speaking of a special group of 'disciples of John'. Remarkably, these writings witness to the continued existence of this distinct group throughout Jesus' ministry. A group of John's adherents continued on to rival followers of Jesus even after John's death. Cf. Acts 18:25; 19:3–4.

### Ministry of Jesus

The reference is to the ministry of Jesus in Matthew 8–9: the blind receive their sight (Mt 9:27–31), the lame walk (Mt 9:2–8), the lepers are cleansed (Mt 8:1–4), the deaf hear (Mt 9:32–34 – *kōphos* meant deaf and/or mute), the dead are raised (Mt 9:18–26) and the poor have good news brought to them (Mt 9:35–38).

### Elijah

Elijah or an Elijah-type figure was widely expected to usher in the end. This was based not only on the spectacular manner of Elijah's departure (2 Kings 2:1–11) but also on prophetic oracles, such as 'Lo, I will send you the prophet Elijah before the great and terrible day of the Lord comes. He will turn the hearts of parents to their children and the hearts of children to their parents, so that I will not come and strike the land with a curse' (Mal 4:5–6); and 'At the appointed time, it is written, you [i.e. Elijah] are destined to calm the wrath of God before it breaks out in fury, to turn the hearts of parents to their children, and to restore the tribes of Jacob' (Sir 48:10). The Elijah identity of John is hinted at in Mark, expressly affirmed by Jesus in Matthew and flatly denied by John himself in the Fourth Gospel. He did cause some anxiety!

## St Paul

From Paul, a slave of Christ Jesus, called to be an apostle, set apart for the gospel of God. This gospel he promised beforehand through his prophets in the holy scriptures, concerning his Son who was a descendant of David with reference to the flesh, who was appointed the Son-of-God-in-power according to the Holy Spirit by the resurrection from the dead, Jesus Christ our Lord. Through him we have received grace and our apostleship to bring about the obedience of faith among all the Gentiles on behalf of his name. You also are among them, called to belong to Jesus Christ. To all those loved by God in Rome, called to be saints: Grace and peace to you from God our Father and the Lord Jesus Christ. (Rom 1:1–7)

## Brief commentary

(V. 2)
'The Messiah' is Matthew's word here – it reminds the readers of Jesus' real identity, still unknown to John the Baptist. Prison: cf. Matthew 14:1–3.

(V. 3)
Given the role and especially the fiery preaching of John, the question is a natural one, as Jesus does not seem to fit the expectation (cf. chapter 3).

(V. 4)
An oblique answer, suggesting, that this exchange is perhaps a later theological clarification of how these two foundational figures related.

(V. 5)
Such deeds may be found in Matthew 8–9, as noted above. Elijah and Elisha did similar deeds of power. Matthew 5–7 and 10 are in the general picture as well.

(V. 6)
The same word is used in the Beatitudes in Matthew 5:1–12. Offence means literally a scandal, a stumbling block Mt (14), Mk (8), Lk (2), Jn (2). Cf. Matthew 13:21 and 15:12. Jesus warns John not to fall himself from faith.

(V. 7)
Rich in rhetorical questions and climax, Jesus identifies John as more than a prophet. The images of reed, robes and palaces may point to Herod Antipas, who put John into prison and whose coins bore a reed.

(V. 9)
'More than a prophet' because, as the last prophet, he ushered in the final age.

(V. 10)
This important citation from Malachi 3:1 is mistakenly cited under Isaiah in Mark 1:2. Cf. also Exodus 23:20.

(V. 11)
'Born of women' covers all humanity. 'Least (in the kingdom)' is an important expression in Matthew 5:19; 25:40, 45. Jesus' own followers are greater than John himself, amazingly.

## Pointers for prayer

a) In response to the question of John, Jesus let his actions speak for him. Some people show by the way they live what it means to be a follower of Jesus. Who has given you such an example? Perhaps there have been times when you have done the same for others.

b) John made a journey of faith from an incomplete knowledge of Jesus to a deeper understanding of who he was. Recall similar steps in your journey of faith.

c) Faith is not primarily about answering abstract theological questions but about living the Gospel. What in your life has helped you to get that sense of perspective?

d) John marked the end of an era, Jesus the beginning of a new one. In our lives how do we honour the past and yet be free to move on into a new era?

## Prayer

*God of glory and compassion, at your touch the wilderness blossoms, broken lives are made whole, and fearful hearts grow strong in faith.*

*Open our eyes to your presence and awaken our hearts to sing your praise.*

*To all who long for your Son's return grant perseverance and patience, that we may announce in word and deed the good news of the kingdom.*

*We ask this through him whose coming is certain, whose day draws near: your Son, our Lord Jesus Christ, who lives and reigns with you in the unity of the Holy Spirit, God for ever and ever. Amen.*

## ✺ Second Reading ✺

**Jas 5:1** *Come now, you rich! Weep and cry aloud over the miseries that are coming on you.* [2]*Your riches have rotted and your clothing has become moth–eaten.* [3]*Your gold and silver have rusted and their rust will be a witness against you. It will consume your flesh like fire. It is in the last days that you have hoarded treasure!* [4]*Look, the pay you have held back from the workers who mowed your fields cries out against you, and the cries of the reapers have reached the ears of the Lord of hosts.* [5]*You have lived indulgently and luxuriously on the earth. You have fattened your hearts in a day of slaughter.* [6]*You have condemned and murdered the righteous person, although he does not resist you.*

[7]So be patient, brothers and sisters, until the Lord's return. Think of how the farmer waits for the precious fruit of the ground and is patient for it until it receives the early and late

rains. [8]You also be patient and strengthen your hearts, for the Lord's return is near. [9]Do not grumble against one another, brothers and sisters, so that you may not be judged. See, the judge stands before the gates! [10]As an example of suffering and patience, brothers and sisters, take the prophets who spoke in the Lord's name. [11]*Think of how we regard as blessed those who have endured. You have heard of Job's endurance and you have seen the Lord's purpose, that the Lord is full of compassion and mercy.* (Jas 5:1–11)

## Initial observations

The full section here really runs from V. 1 to V. 11 (the additional verses are included above in italics). The excerpt is very suitable for Advent. This is the only time these verses are read in the entire three-year cycle of readings.

## Kind of writing

Attempts to identify the kind of writing are quite varied. It may very well be a letter, given that letters at the time took many forms. More precise categories include moral discourse, a baptismal catechism and Christian wisdom.

There seems to be no agreement on the outline or structure of James. Eugene Boring offers the following outline:

| | |
|---|---|
| 1:1 | Salutation |
| 1:2–27 | Perspectives on Christian Character |
| 2:1–13 | Christian morals and the Law |
| 2:14–26 | Faith and works |
| 3:1–12 | Responsible speech |
| 3:13–4:12 | Christians and conflict |
| 4:13–5:6 | Concerning wealth |
| 5:7–20 | Life within the community |

The reading, Vs 7–10, is marked by no fewer than *five* imperatives. In the previous verses, there are severe warnings against the rich. In the second part, the tone changes to instruction for life within the community.

## Context in the community

The community for which this letter is written is unclear. The writer addresses himself to the twelve tribes in the Dispersion (Jas 1:1). This could mean Jews *outside* Palestine or, if the writer is thinking of the 'true Israel', Christians anywhere in the inhabited world.

As for the writer, there are five people called James in the New Testament. Only two are potential candidates for author: *James*, son of Zebedee and brother of John or *James* the brother of the Lord. The former was killed in AD44 by Agrippa I. The latter, according to Josephus was stoned in AD62 or AD69. There are difficulties identifying either of these with the author: the excellent Greek, the use of rhetoric, the absence of reference to Jesus (named only twice in Jas 1:1; 2:1) and finally the address to the diaspora.

## Related passages

> Jesus also said, 'The kingdom of God is as if someone would scatter seed on the ground, and would sleep and rise night and day, and the seed would sprout and grow, he does not know how. The earth produces of itself, first the stalk, then the head, then the full grain in the head. But when the grain is ripe, at once he goes in with his sickle, because the harvest has come.' (Mk 4:26–29)

> And may the Lord cause you to increase and abound in love for one another and for all, just as we do for you, so that your hearts are strengthened in holiness to be blameless before our God and Father at the coming of our Lord Jesus with all his saints. (1 Thess 3:12–13)

## Brief commentary

(V. 7)
Patience is a Christian virtue across the New Testament: Romans 2:4; 9:22; 1 Peter 3:20; 2 Peter 3:15. The 'coming' is literally the *parousia* (see Mt 24:3, 27; 1 Cor 15:23; 1 Thess 2:19; 4:15; 5:23; 2 Thess 2:1; 2

Pet 1:16; 3:4; 1 Jn 2:28). The NRSV 'beloved ' is literally *adelphoi*, i.e. brothers and sisters, correctly rendered in the NET. The image of the farmer recalls a parable of Jesus unique to Mark (see above). On the proverbial early and late rains see Deuteronomy 11:14; Jeremiah 5:24; Hosea 6:3; Joel 2:23.

(V. 8)
On the strengthening of heart, see 1 Thessalonians 3:13 above. The same word is used for the nearness of the kingdom in Mark: 'The time is fulfilled, and the kingdom of God has come near; repent, and believe in the good news.' (Mk 1:15).

(V. 9)
This is completely normal, of course (and alas). The writer already alluded to this in the letter: 'Do not speak against one another, brothers and sisters. He who speaks against a fellow believer or judges a fellow believer speaks against the law and judges the law. But if you judge the law, you are not a doer of the law but its judge. But there is only one who is lawgiver and judge – the one who is able to save and destroy. On the other hand, who are you to judge your neighbour?' (Jas 4:11–12). 'Door' is an echo of early passages in the New Testament such as: 'So also you, when you see these things happening, know that he is near, right at the door' (Mk 13:29).

(V. 10)
No specific examples are given but see the following: Hebrews 11:32–38; 1 Maccabees 2:49–61; Sirach 44:16–50:21.

## Pointers for prayer

a) In your own life at the moment, where you do find the need for patience? Is there also a spiritual *im*patience to be acknowledged?

b) The example of the farming is familiar and inspiring: certain things simply take (their own) time. What has helped you appreciate this word of wisdom?

c) Are there particular examples of patience who have encouraged you in your own own life? Give thanks to God for them all.

## Prayer

*Give us the wisdom which comes from you, O Lord,*
*that we may know how to endure and when to be patient.*
*In your eyes, there is a time for everything.*
*Help us to live expectantly in the present moment that we may be found*
*watchful in prayer, strong in love and faithful to the breaking of the bread.*
*Through Christ our Lord. Amen.*

## 🍃 First Reading 🍃

Isa 35:1  Let the desert and dry region be happy;
let the wilderness rejoice and bloom like a lily!
² Let it richly bloom;
let it rejoice and shout with delight!
It is given the grandeur of Lebanon,
the splendour of Carmel and Sharon.
They will see the grandeur of the Lord,
the splendour of our God.
³ Strengthen the hands that have gone limp,
steady the knees that shake!
⁴ Tell those who panic,
'Be strong! Do not fear!
Look, your God comes to avenge!
With divine retribution he comes to deliver you. '
⁵ Then blind eyes will open,
deaf ears will hear.
⁶ Then the lame will leap like a deer,
the mute tongue will shout for joy;
*for water will flow in the desert,*

    *streams in the wilderness.*
7  *The dry soil will become a pool of water,*
    *the parched ground springs of water.*
    *Where jackals once lived and sprawled out,*
    *grass, reeds, and papyrus will grow.*
8  *A thoroughfare will be there—*
    *it will be called the Way of Holiness.*
    *The unclean will not travel on it;*
    *it is reserved for those authorised to use it—*
    *fools will not stray into it.*
9  *No lions will be there,*
    *no ferocious wild animals will be on it—*
    *they will not be found there.*
    *Those delivered from bondage will travel on it,*
10  those whom the LORD has ransomed will return that way.
    They will enter Zion with a happy shout.
    Unending joy will crown them,
    happiness and joy will overwhelm them;
    grief and suffering will disappear.

## Initial Observations

Our reading captures the mood of Gaudete Sunday. The festive note within Advent is marked by the lighting of the third rose candle on the traditional wreath.

## Kind of Writing

Some of the very best biblical poetry is to be found in Job and in Second Isaiah, including this chapter here. The lines are more or less all in parallel, showing that 'uneasy synonymity' which gives biblical poetry its peculiar energy.

At a literary level, we make note that striking combination of metaphors from nature, forensic vocabulary and 'body language': *nature* (wilderness, dry land, desert, crocus, blossom, Lebanon, Carmel, Sharon); *forensic* (vengeance, recompense, save); *body* (hands, knees, heart, eyes, ears, lame, tongue).

## Origin of the reading

Generally, scholars would hold that both chapter 34 and chapter 35 reflect the later experience of the great exile in Babylon and these chapters should therefore be located in Second Isaiah. V. 6a makes the parallel with the Gospel stand out. Then we move forward to the marvellous vision of V. 10.

## Related passages

Get you up to a high mountain, O Zion, herald of good tidings; lift up your voice with strength, O Jerusalem, herald of good tidings, lift it up, do not fear; say to the cities of Judah, 'Here is your God!' See, the Lord GOD comes with might, and his arm rules for him; his reward is with him, and his recompense before him. (Isaiah 40:9–10) See also: Isaiah 41:18–19 and Isaiah 51:3.

## Brief commentary

(V. 1)
Three terms are used for the land: wilderness, dry land and the Arabah. All three refer to the great rift of the Jordan, leading to the Gulf of Aqaba. The landscape looks forbidding but is essentially fertile when rains comes, which is seldom. The crocus is a symbol of the transformation that occurs when it does actually rain.

(V. 2)
The glory of Lebanon is its majestic covering of trees. Carmel and Sharon are coastal areas known for fertility, fields and flowers. The glory of the Lord is an extensive motif in Isaiah.

> Then the glory of the LORD shall be revealed, and all people
> shall see it together, for the mouth of the LORD has spoken.
> (Isa 40:5)

(Vs 3–6b)
Perhaps we are meant to imagine a pilgrim group, making its way to Jerusalem. Humanity, in all its frailty, is well represented.

The time of terrible devastation and punishment is coming to an end. I replied, 'How long, sovereign master?' He said, 'Until cities are in ruins and unpopulated, and houses are uninhabited, and the land is ruined and devastated, and the LORD has sent the people off to a distant place, and the very heart of the land is completely abandoned. Even if only a tenth of the people remain in the land, it will again be destroyed, like one of the large sacred trees or an Asherah pole, when a sacred pillar on a high place is thrown down. That sacred pillar symbolises the special chosen family.' (Isa 6:11–13)

(V. 10a)

The bodily metaphors are dropped and replaced by the language of redemption and salvation. The 'redeemed of the Lord' make their return to Zion:

Zion will be freed by justice, and her returnees by righteousness. (Isa 1:27)

Why does no one challenge me when I come? Why does no one respond when I call? Is my hand too weak to deliver you? Do I lack the power to rescue you? Look, with a mere shout I can dry up the sea; I can turn streams into a desert, so the fish rot away and die from lack of water. (Isa 50:2)

(V. 10b)

The tone at the end is quite ecstatic. It no accident that this very evocative text was set to such deeply felt music by Johannes Brahms, in his *German Requiem*, marking the death his mother.

## Pointers for prayer

a) The vision is one of home coming and deep fulfillment. This could be true literally for each of us at some point in our story. It could also be a way of speaking of our spiritual 'flying home to God' (cf. Patrick Kavanagh's 'Beyond the Headlines').

b) Can I name my own needs using the metaphors of the poetry: how am I deaf, lame etc.?

## Prayer

*God of all our joy, you call us all to life in abundance*
*and to deep inner joy in knowing you.*
*At times we are deaf, lame, unable to speak.*
*Open our ears that we may walk again the path of life*
*and praise your name. Through Christ our Lord. Amen.*

# Chapter 4

## Advent 4A

## Thought for the day

In a culture where God is, evidently, absent, it may sound strange to hear words such as 'Do not be afraid' and 'God is with us'. Such assurances are at the heart our biblical faith from beginning to end. Everyone who is anyone in the Bible is told at some point not to be afraid. And the assurance 'I will be with you' is also found throughout starting with the very name of God in Exodus 3:14, *I am who I am*. The God – *in whom we live and move and have our being* – is there all along, whether we are aware of it or not. Faith is the moment of discovery and recognition.

## Prayer

*You are with us always: you are with us in creation in all its splendour,*
*in our fellow human beings in all their generosity,*
*you are with us in the quiet where we are alone with you.*
*Help ask to be present to you who are always with us.*
*Through Christ our Lord. Amen.*

## 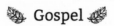 Gospel

**Mt 1:18** Now the birth of Jesus the Messiah took place in this way. When his mother Mary had been engaged to Joseph, but before they lived together, she was found to be with child from the Holy Spirit. [19]Her husband Joseph, being a righteous man and unwilling to expose her to public disgrace, planned to dismiss her quietly. [20]But just when he had resolved to do this, an angel of the Lord appeared to him in a dream and said, 'Joseph, son of David, do not be afraid to take Mary as your wife, for the child conceived in her is from the Holy Spirit. [21]She will bear a son, and you are to name him Jesus, for he will save his people from their sins.' [22]All this took place to fulfil what had been spoken by the Lord through the prophet: [23]'Look, the virgin shall conceive and bear a son, and they shall name him Emmanuel', which means, 'God is with us.' [24]When Joseph awoke from sleep, he did as the angel of the Lord commanded him; he took her as his wife.

## Initial observations

Advent 4 takes us back to the conception of Jesus. The story in Matthew 1:18–24 (annunciation to Joseph) corresponds to Luke 1:26–38 (annunciation to Mary). The excerpt omits, for liturgical reasons, the next verse, which reads 'but [he] had no marital relations with her until she had borne a son; and he named him Jesus' (Mt 1:25). This is an accurate, if slightly awkward, translation.

## Old Testament background

### *Joseph*

The name Joseph reminds the aware bible reader of another Joseph in the Book of Genesis. That Joseph was a dreamer, threatened by his brothers, who went down to Egypt. Because of his position, Egypt became a place of refuge for his family. The character of our Joseph and the narrative surrounding him all come from Genesis 37–50.

### *Divorce*

Divorce was allowed by inference in Deuteronomy 24:1–4, although no legislation formally permitted it. The rabbis discussed 'warmly' the conditions under which a man might divorce his wife and opinions varied as to the severity of the causes.

## Son of David

The relationship with David immediately calls to mind the guarantee and promise to the house of David made by the prophet Nathan in 2 Samuel 7 and the prayer version of it in Psalm 89. David was the anointed shepherd king of Israel – language significant in Matthew. In the centuries before Jesus' birth, people's hopes focused on a restoration of the kingdom of David, as a sign of God's continued faithfulness to his people.

## Jesus

Jesus is the Greek for Joshua, the name of Moses' successor, who actually led the people into the Promised Land. The name comes Hebrew/Aramaic and means 'YHWH is salvation' or 'YHWH saves/ has saved'. Messiah or Christ is not found in the Hebrew Bible pointing to an expected end-time agent of God's salvation. That language and expectation developed in the last two centuries before the birth of Jesus.

## Prophecy

The promise in Isaiah 7:14 is read as a messianic prophecy. In its original context, this text promised a successor to King Ahaz, conceived and born in the usual way. The Hebrew says *'alma'*, which could be a young woman and/or a virgin. The early Greek version of the Old Testament (the Septuagint) used the word 'virgin', taken up here by Matthew because it fits with his account of Jesus' virginal conception.

# Kind of writing

## Dreams

For communication in a dream, the clear prototypes are Jacob (and his famous ladder) and Joseph (with the coat of many colours). Otherwise, the Bible is hesitant, not to say suspicious, of divination by dreams.

## Annunciation-type Stories

These stories show the following pattern. (1) Appearance of an angel; (2) fear and/or prostration; (3) message; (4) objection; (5) sign. In the

Old Testament: Ishmael (Gen 16:7–12), Isaac (Gen 17:1–21; 18:1–12); Samson (Judg 13:3–21). In the New Testament: John the Baptist (Lk 1:11–20); Jesus (Lk 1:26–38). Our version in Matthew is missing one element, the sign: the angel comes in a dream and there is a message. Implied are (a) fear – 'Do not be afraid' – and (b) an objection – Joseph wants a divorce and the angel somehow knows this.

*Fulfilment of Prophecy*

Fives times in chapters 1–2, Matthew says the events described fulfilled something from the Hebrew Bible. The purpose is to underline continuity – i.e. God's fidelity, even in the unexpected context of a Jewish-Christian community of faith.

## New Testament foreground

*Jesus' Name*

Matthew is the only Gospel to give the meaning of the name Jesus. Intriguingly, he more than doubles the occurrence of the name Jesus in the Passion Narrative from seventeen times to forty, perhaps because he wants us to hear the etymology and its meaning ringing in our ears as we hear the story of Jesus' death.

*Emmanuel (literally, God with us)*

As is well-known, the Gospel's first mention of Jesus includes this name and this Gospel closes with a final evocation: 'And remember, *I am with you* always, to the end of the age' (Mt 28:20).

## St Paul

> But when the appropriate time had come, God sent out his Son, born of a woman, born under the law, to redeem those who were under the law, so that we may be adopted as sons with full rights. And because you are sons, God sent the Spirit of his Son into our hearts, who calls 'Abba! Father!' So you are no longer a slave but a son, and if you are a son, then you are also an heir through God. (Gal 4:4–7)

## Brief commentary

In a discrete way, using narrative, Matthew achieves a tremendous theology of the child to be born: Son of David, the new Joshua, Saviour, God-with-us, all brought by the Holy Spirit and divine intervention.

(V. 18)
The virginal conception of Jesus is a tradition that antedates both Matthew and Luke, as they both contain it seemingly independently of each other. A conception outside of wedlock serves to make that lack of human causality apparent. The Holy Spirit as the agent is found also in Luke.

(V. 19)
In this way, the good character of Joseph is affirmed.

(V. 20)
Here we have the typical vocabulary of annunciation scenes. By means of 'Son of David' the legal paternity is traced to the husband. 'Do not be afraid' is one of the most common expressions across the whole Bible. Anyone who is anyone in the biblical narrative both needs and receives this reassurance. The fear intended is not emotional fright but, so to speak, ontological dread, awe, before the mystery of God.

(V. 21)
Saving people from the sins is part of Matthew's theology of the cross. That is why he increases so much the occurrence of the name Jesus in his Passion Narrative.

(V. 22)
As elsewhere, Matthew makes us of a citation for proof of veracity and to underline continuity with earlier covenants.

(V. 23)
Virginity (in the biblical world, essential before marriage but catastrophic if life-long) is a symbol of unrealised potential – exactly that period

of longing after disappropriation and disappointment envisaged in the genealogy in Matthew as the setting for coming of the Messiah.

(V. 24)
Joseph is always obedient to his dreams – see Matthew 2:13 and 2:19.

## Pointers for prayer

As we move into prayer on the passage, we move from consideration of the mystery of how 'God with us' was revealed to the world in the person of Jesus two thousand years ago, to a reflection on how we become aware of 'God with us' now in our daily lives.

a) It took some time for Joseph to accept the fact that in Mary there truly was Emmanuel – God with us. God is with us now, but at times we struggle to perceive God's presence. Where have you unexpectedly discovered the presence of 'God with you'? Recall those experiences and give thanks.

b) Joseph was confused and uncertain about what he should do. It was difficult for him to discern what his next step should be. Perhaps you have also had to make difficult journeys on the way to some decisions or commitments. Recall that journey and the moments when it became clear to you what was being asked of you. Give thanks for the angels who helped you along the way.

c) Mary bore Jesus within her, unseen to all, and unacknowledged by most. In Joseph she found one who believed in the treasure that she bore. We can be bearers of Jesus to others, and they to us. When have you been a bearer of Jesus to another? Who has been that to you?

d) The experience of having a gift that others do not see or recognise can be painful and isolating. Then someone comes, like Joseph to Mary, who gets to believe in what we have to offer. Has that happened to you? What was it like?

# Prayer

*Eternal God, in the psalms of David, in the words of the prophets, in the dream of Joseph, your promise is spoken. At last, in the womb of the Virgin Mary, your Word takes flesh.*

*Teach us to welcome Jesus, the promised Emmanuel, and to preach the good news of his coming that every age may know him as the source of redemption and grace.*

*We ask this through him whose coming is certain, whose day draws near: your Son, our Lord Jesus Christ, who lives and reigns with you in the unity of the Holy Spirit, God for ever and ever. Amen.*

## 🌿 Second Reading 🌿

**Rom 1:1** From Paul, a slave of Christ Jesus, called to be an apostle, set apart for the gospel of God. ²This gospel he promised beforehand through his prophets in the holy scriptures, ³concerning his Son who was a descendant of David with reference to the flesh, ⁴who was appointed the Son-of-God-in-power according to the Holy Spirit by the resurrection from the dead, Jesus Christ our Lord. ⁵Through him we have received grace and our apostleship to bring about the obedience of faith among all the Gentiles on behalf of his name. ⁶You also are among them, called to belong to Jesus Christ. ⁷To all those loved by God in Rome, called to be saints: Grace and peace to you from God our Father and the Lord Jesus Christ! (Rom 1:1–7)

## Initial observations

The reading might seem a strange one – the opening salutation from the letter to the Romans – but it is very rich and, in reality, very appropriate. The surface link is the mention of David on all three readings. It is, in many ways, an implied summary of the content of Romans and an anticipation of Paul's advice to them all, both Jews and Gentiles.

## Kind of writing

All the letters start with some such salutation, through none is so elaborate as this greeting in Romans. After all, Paul could have written 'From Paul, a slave of Christ Jesus, to all those loved by God in Rome, called to be saints: Grace and peace to you from God our Father and the Lord Jesus Christ!' The longer salutation incorporates a summary of the Good News, with its roots in Judaism, as well as presentation of the apostolate of Paul, sent, significantly, to all the Gentiles, including those in Rome.

## Context in the community

The context is a split in the Roman houses churches, along the lines of Jews and Gentiles. The issue at stake is how much of the previous, Jewish tradition to retain. The Jews could claim a greater fidelity – and regard the Gentiles as failing to do what God asked through Moses. The Gentiles could claim a greater freedom in Christ – and regard the Jews as failing to recognise the consequences of the Christ event. A division along these lines, at the heart of the empire, threatened the core of the Pauline Gospel: the extension of God's grace to all without distinction. Hence, Paul writes to a church he did *not* found and had not yet even visited.

## Related passages

### Greeting

> From Paul, called to be an apostle of Christ Jesus by the will of God, and Sosthenes, our brother, to the church of God that is in Corinth, to those who are sanctified in Christ Jesus, and called to be saints, with all those in every place who call on the name of our Lord Jesus Christ, their Lord and ours. Grace and peace to you from God our Father and the Lord Jesus Christ! (1 Cor 1:1–3)

*Gospel*

> For I am not ashamed of the gospel, for it is God's power for salvation to everyone who believes, to the Jew first and also to the Greek. For the righteousness of God is revealed in the gospel from faith to faith, just as it is written, 'The righteous by faith will live.' (Rom 1:16–17)

> For since in the wisdom of God the world by its wisdom did not know God, God was pleased to save those who believe by the foolishness of preaching. For Jews demand miraculous signs and Greeks ask for wisdom, but we preach about a crucified Christ, a stumbling block to Jews and foolishness to Gentiles. But to those who are called, both Jews and Greeks, Christ is the power of God and the wisdom of God. For the foolishness of God is wiser than human wisdom, and the weakness of God is stronger than human strength. (1 Cor 1:21–25)

## Brief commentary

(V. 1)

Slave (or servant) placed Paul immediately in a context of obedience which would appeal to the faithful Jewish Christians. Apostle: he claims his own authority as in the letter to the Galatians. Set apart: firstly, for a special responsibility to the Gentiles (see V. 5); secondly, 'apart' (*aphōrismenos*) may be a play on word with 'pharisee'. Identifying with a group very committed to the Law would also appeal to Christians of Jewish origin. At the same time, 'set apart' indicates something new and distinctive. Gospel: in the teaching of Paul this means the proclamation of the cross and resurrection. Occasionally, Paul offers a short definition of sorts. See above: Romans 1:16–17 and 1 Corinthians 1:21–25. Cf. Romans 1:1, 9, 16; 2:16; 10:16; 11:28; 15:16, 19; 16:25.

(V. 2)

Thus Paul affirms the Jewishness of the roots of Gospel, an important affirmation for the Jewish Christians. In Paul's view, the Gospel is not the teaching *of* Jesus but the teaching *about* Jesus with his death and resurrection at the heart of it all. See above Romans 1:16–17 and 1 Corinthians 1:21–25.

(V. 3)

The Jewish descent of Jesus comes up for an impassioned mention in Romans 9:1–5 and throughout Romans 9–11. Descent *from David* links Jesus to God's fidelity to the Israelites *across time*.

(V. 4)

In the language of later heresy, this verse could sound 'adoptionist'. It is somewhat unclear whether Paul is offering his own teaching or whether he is citing a formula current among the Roman Christians of Jewish origin. The Holy Spirit is hugely important in Romans. For example in Romans 5:1–5 and throughout chapter 8.

(V. 5)

Romans is written to a community which Paul had *never* been to, much less founded. Hence his need to account for his apostleship and his writing to them at all. He is called to *all* the Gentiles, who therefore include the Roman Christians of Gentile origin.

(V. 6)

This generic claim takes in both Jewish and Gentile disciples. Paul will draw out the practical implications of belonging in Romans 12:1–15:6 and, in particular, the practice of tolerance.

(V. 7)

In spite of their differences, all in the Roman house churches are loved by God – the very foundation of their being disciples in the first place. Note the repetition of 'all'. They too are called to holiness and for that they need grace (the sense of giftedness) and peace (the practice is reconciliation).

## Pointers for prayer

a) Paul offers a summary, with a special emphasis on the roots of the faith. How would you name the roots of *your* faith?

b) Both Paul and the Romans are *called* to holiness and apostleship. What is your own calling as a disciple?

## Prayer

*God of every grace and blessing, help us to know the
depth of your gift and love in Christ.
Help us to recognise and set aside the difficulties that keep us apart.
Through Christ our Lord. Amen.*

## ✥ First Reading ✥

**Isa 7:10** The Lord again spoke to Ahaz: [11]'Ask for a confirming sign from the Lord your God. You can even ask for something miraculous.' [12]But Ahaz responded, 'I don't want to ask; I don't want to put the Lord to a test.' [13]So Isaiah replied, 'Pay attention, family of David. Do you consider it too insignificant to try the patience of men? Is that why you are also trying the patience of my God? [14]For this reason the sovereign master himself will give you a confirming sign. Look, this young woman is about to conceive and will give birth to a son. You, young woman, will name him Immanuel. [15]*He will eat sour milk and honey, which will help him know how to reject evil and choose what is right.* 16 *Here is why this will be so: Before the child knows how to reject evil and choose what is right, the land whose two kings you fear will be desolate.'*

## Initial observations

The reading is a perfect match for the Gospel. At the same time, it ought to be interpreted in its own context and time as well as looking backwards in the light of the Christian use of the passage.

## Kind of writing

Technically, this is a sign narrative. In the Bible, it is not usual for signs to be given without a specific request. The text is in two parts. Part I (Vs 10–13) is a dialogue about the sign. Part II (Vs 14–16) is the actual sign itself. The lectionary leaves out V. 15 and V. 16, probably to close the reading with the word Emmanuel, God-with-us.

## Origin of the reading

As noted earlier in Advent, our reading is from first Isaiah, that is, chapters 1–39. The first section of Isaiah runs from chapters 1–12.

1–12: condemnation and salvation; Davidic king; Assyria as God's instrument.

It is noticeable that the passage starts, in Hebrew, with 'again'. This places it in the context Isaiah 7:1–8:18, that is during the Syro–Ephraimite war. The message in the early part of chapter 7 is a word from the Lord to resist the advice of battle-hungry generals and to sit tight.

> Tell him, 'Make sure you stay calm! Don't be afraid! Don't be intimidated by these two stubs of smoking logs, or by the raging anger of Rezin, Syria, and the son of Remaliah.' (Isa 7:4)

> Ephraim's leader is Samaria, and Samaria's leader is the son of Remaliah. If your faith does not remain firm, then you will not remain secure. ' (Isaiah 7:9)

The oracle we are reading follows on as a second assurance to Ahaz and this time it takes the form of dynastic continuity and fertility.

The contextual meaning, therefore, is that a woman of the royal house will have a child and God's promise through Nathan to David will be sustained.

## Related passages

> At that time King Rezin of Syria and King Pekah son of Remaliah of Israel attacked Jerusalem. They besieged Ahaz, but were unable to conquer him. (2 Kings 16:5)

Cf. Isaiah 7:1–2.

## Brief commentary

(V. 10)
This is a second word and a second encouragement to hold fast to the policy of loyalty to Assyria.

(V. 11)
Prophets offer signs so that the recipient may know that God is fulfilling his word. For example, Samuel offers a sign to Saul:
> 'When these signs have taken place, do whatever your hand finds to do, for God will be with you. You will go down to Gilgal before me. I am going to join you there to offer burnt offerings and to make peace offerings. You should wait for seven days, until I arrive and tell you what to do.' As Saul turned to leave Samuel, God changed his inmost person. All these signs happened on that very day. (1 Sam 10:7–9)

(V. 12)
Why does Ahaz react so cautiously, even negatively? Because seeking a sign could be interpreted to mean lack of faith, a kind of testing of God. For example:
> So the people contended with Moses, and they said, 'Give us water to drink!' Moses said to them, 'Why do you contend with me? Why do you test the LORD?' (Ex 17:2)

'You must not put the LORD your God to the test as you did at Massah.' (Deut 6:16)

Yet they challenged and defied the sovereign God, and did not obey his commands (Ps 78:56)

So, it seems that Ahaz refuses not because of disrespect but on account of his cautious piety.

### (V. 13)
It is made explicit that the Lord had been speaking throughout not directly to but through Isaiah. The address changes to the second person plural. The plural fits the wider address 'House of Israel'.

Ahaz is strongly condemned in Kings and Chronicles for dithering. He did weary his people, even at this early stage. He may also have wearied God by distancing himself from the religious reassurance / sign which would have helped.

### (V. 14)
In the historical context, a miraculous conception is not in view. The young woman is unmarried and therefore the Greek translation 'virgin' is not inaccurate. The birth, however, is a sign of God's continued presence and action, as is every birth. Hence the name: 'immanu' means 'with us' and 'el' means 'God'.

### (Vs 15–16)
Opaque to us, these verses have a simple, political meaning. When the child grows up, the present crisis will be resolved.

## Pointers for prayer

a) A child is always a blessing and at our own birth each one of us was a blessing to our parents. Children are a blessing to us too. Prayer of praise and thanksgiving for the gift of life and the wonder of being.

b) The reading invites us to see the hand of God in all that happens to us. He is our Emmanuel, God-with-us always, in whom we live and move and have our being.

## Prayer

*God, giver of every good gift, origin of all we have are: to you we pray.*
*We thank you for the wonder of our being;*
*we thank you for the hunger of the heart that draws us to you;*
*we thank you for your continued presence and action in our lives.*
*Bless us as we prepare to mark the birth of you Son,*
*Emmanuel, Jesus Christ our Lord. Amen.*

# Chapter 5

# Christmas Eve Vigil Mass (ABC)

## Thought for the day

Tracing origins has always been of interest and nowadays it is possible to have a sample of your DNA tested to find out what kind of genetic mix you are, but the great message of the Gospel is that our past does not always have to stalk us – there is total forgiveness and even amnesia in God: 'I, I am the one who blots out your rebellious deeds for my sake; your sins I do not remember' (Isa 43:25).

## Prayer

*Help us to accept from you, God, a new name, a new reality in Christ that we may know your forgiveness and love and be set free from our past sins and faults. Through Christ our Lord.*

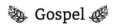 ## Gospel

**Mt 1:1** An account of the genealogy of Jesus the Messiah, the son of David, the son of Abraham.

²Abraham was the father of Isaac, and Isaac the father of Jacob, and Jacob the father of Judah and his brothers, ³and Judah the father of Perez and Zerah by Tamar, and Perez the father of Hezron, and Hezron the father of Aram, ⁴and Aram the father of Aminadab, and Aminadab the father of

Nahshon, and Nahshon the father of Salmon, [5]and Salmon the father of Boaz by Rahab, and Boaz the father of Obed by Ruth, and Obed the father of Jesse, [6]and Jesse the father of King David.

And David was the father of Solomon by the wife of Uriah, [7]and Solomon the father of Rehoboam, and Rehoboam the father of Abijah, and Abijah the father of Asaph, [8]and Asaph the father of Jehoshaphat, and Jehoshaphat the father of Joram, and Joram the father of Uzziah, [9]and Uzziah the father of Jotham, and Jotham the father of Ahaz, and Ahaz the father of Hezekiah, [10]and Hezekiah the father of Manasseh, and Manasseh the father of Amos, and Amos the father of Josiah, [11]and Josiah the father of Jechoniah and his brothers, at the time of the deportation to Babylon.

[12]And after the deportation to Babylon: Jechoniah was the father of Salathiel, and Salathiel the father of Zerubbabel, [13]and Zerubbabel the father of Abiud, and Abiud the father of Eliakim, and Eliakim the father of Azor, [14]and Azor the father of Zadok, and Zadok the father of Achim, and Achim the father of Eliud, [15]and Eliud the father of Eleazar, and Eleazar the father of Matthan, and Matthan the father of Jacob, [16]and Jacob the father of Joseph the husband of Mary, of whom Jesus was born, who is called the Messiah.

[17]So all the generations from Abraham to David are fourteen generations; and from David to the deportation to Babylon, fourteen generations; and from the deportation to Babylon to the Messiah, fourteen generations.

[18]Now the birth of Jesus the Messiah took place in this way. When his mother Mary had been engaged to Joseph, but before they lived together, she was found to be with child from the Holy Spirit. [19]Her husband Joseph, being a righteous man and unwilling to expose her to public disgrace, planned to

dismiss her quietly. [20]But just when he had resolved to do this, an angel of the Lord appeared to him in a dream and said, 'Joseph, son of David, do not be afraid to take Mary as your wife, for the child conceived in her is from the Holy Spirit. [21]She will bear a son, and you are to name him Jesus, for he will save his people from their sins'. [22]All this took place to fulfil what had been spoken by the Lord through the prophet:

[23]'Look, the virgin shall conceive and bear a son, and they shall name him Emmanuel', which means, 'God is with us.' [24]When Joseph awoke from sleep, he did as the angel of the Lord commanded him; he took her as his wife, [25]but had no marital relations with her until she had borne a son; and he named him Jesus.

## Initial observations

There is no doubt that the (optional) genealogy is disconcerting for the modern reader/listener. Nevertheless it was immensely significant for Matthew. By means of it, the evangelist was able to embed the story of Jesus in the story of God's first chosen people. It is likely that Matthew's community had just broken away from 'the synagogue'. At the same time, this community claimed to be in continuity with God's past disclosure to the Jewish people, now brought to completion in Jesus the Messiah. In particular, the figure of Moses dominates Matthew's presentation of Jesus.

## Kind of writing

*Genealogy*

The genealogy in Matthew is divided in three grand periods: from Abraham to David ('promise'), from David to the exile in Babylon ('possession and loss') and from the exile to Jesus the Messiah ('longing'). Jesus is to be understood in the light of this great narrative arc from the story of Israel. In case we missed the pattern, the author draws our attention to it in V. 17 as follows: 'So all the generations from Abraham to David are fourteen generations; and from David to the deportation to Babylon, fourteen generations; and from the deportation to Babylon to the Messiah, fourteen generations' (Mt 1:17). The emphasis on the number fourteen serves two purposes. Firstly, it indicates divine purpose and the reader is to understand that something is coming to completion at this point. Secondly, the ancient Israelites, like the ancient Romans, used letters for numbers. It so happens that the consonants of the name David, DVD, were equivalent to the number fourteen. The link to David takes us directly to God's faithfulness. God promised to be faithful to David and his dynasty, a faithfulness which comes to a climax in Jesus, a descendent of David.

*Annunciation*

The annunciation-type story shows a pattern we will recognise from the appearance of part of this pattern in Matthew 1:18–24: (1) appearance of an angel; (2) fear and/or prostration; (3) reassurance ('do not fear'); (4) message; (5) objection; (6) a sign is given.

The pattern is familiar from the Old Testament (Ishmael in Gen 16:7–12, Isaac in Gen 17:1–21; 18:1–12 and Samson in Judg 13:3–21) but is only partially present here in Matthew.

## Old Testament background

The broad Old Testament story is presented schematically using the device of fourteen generations, taking us from Abraham, through David and the exile to the time of Jesus. In antiquity, evidently, people were unaware of ovulation. As a result, women were omitted from genealogies. As a result the inclusion of women here is especially significant. Each one has a story.

a) Tamar: Genesis 38
b) Rahab: Joshua 2–6
c) Ruth: the Book of Ruth
d) Wife of Uriah (Bethsheba): 2 Samuel 11–12

All four are in some sense irregular, either sexually and/or as foreigners. They prepare for the great 'irregularity' of the virginal conception and look forward, at the same time, to the inclusion of the Gentiles in the new covenant in Jesus. Sinners likewise have a role in God's plan: three of the women are technically sinners but so are lots of the men, such as David himself and Solomon.

a) Joseph: as we saw in chapter four the name Joseph reminds the aware bible reader of another Joseph in the Book of Genesis.

b) Divorce was allowed by inference in Deuteronomy 24:1–4, although no biblical legislation formally permitted it.

c) Son of David: the relationship with David immediately calls to mind the guarantee and promise to the house of David made by the prophet Nathan in 2 Samuel 7 and the prayer version of it in Psalm 89.

d) Jesus is the Greek for Joshua, the name of Moses' successor, who actually led the people into the promised land. The name comes Hebrew/Aramaic and means 'YHWH is salvation' or 'YHWH saves/has saved'.

e) The promise in Isaiah 7:14 is read as a messianic prophecy. In its original context, this text promised a successor to King Ahaz, born in the normal way.

f) Communication in a dream: the clear prototypes are Jacob (and his famous ladder) and Joseph (with his coat of many colours). (should this appear in kind of writing section?)

## New Testament foreground

Now the eleven disciples went to Galilee, to the mountain to which Jesus had directed them. When they saw him, they worshiped him; but some doubted. And Jesus came and said to them, 'All authority in heaven and on earth has been given to me. Go therefore and make disciples of all nations, baptising them in the name of the Father and of the Son and of the Holy Spirit, and teaching them to obey everything that

> I have commanded you. And remember, *I am with you always,* *to the end of the age.*' (Mt 28:16–20, emphasis added)

## St Paul

> For this reason it is by faith so that it may be by grace, with the result that the promise may be certain to all the descendants – not only to those who are under the law, but also to those who have the faith of Abraham, who is the father of us all (as it is written, 'I have made you the father of many nations'). He is our father in the presence of God whom he believed – the God who makes the dead alive and summons the things that do not yet exist as though they already do. Against hope Abraham believed in hope with the result that he became the father of many nations according to the pronouncement, 'so will your descendants be'. Without being weak in faith, he considered his own body as dead (because he was about one hundred years old) and the deadness of Sarah's womb. He did not waver in unbelief about the promise of God but was strengthened in faith, giving glory to God. (Rom 4:16–20)

## Brief commentary

Because of the extended Old Testament background, only selected verses will be commented.

(V. 1)
The first verse anticipates the three-fold pattern, pointing to Jesus.

(V. 6)
People did look back on the time of David as a sort of golden age and many hopes were expressed using Davidic imagery from the Psalms and other documents.

(V. 11)
The Babylonian Exile was a watershed in the history and imagination

of the Jewish people. It will be referred to again in the slaughter of the innocents in Matthew 2:17–18.

(V. 16)

The pairing of a later Jacob with the later Joseph intentionally echoes the great patriarch, the father of the twelve sons of Jacob, the progenitors of twelve tribes of Israel.

(V. 17)

The writer insistently draws our attention to the pattern of fourteen. It may be significant that the consonants of the name David had the numerical value of fourteen.

(V. 18)

Mary was not descended from all these people but Joseph, as the legal father of Jesus, was. Betrothal was almost marriage; it was quite in order, therefore, to speak of divorce. The virginal conception is found also in Luke's account of the conception of Jesus.

(V. 20)

Do not be afraid is a key element in the Annunciation-type scene.

(V. 21)

As explained above the name Jesus means YHWH saves. In antiquity, names were regarded as key to the person's identity and mission (cf. *nomen omen*).

(Vs 22–23)

Matthew peppers his account with fulfilment citations, of which this is the first. Originally, Isaiah 7:14 (in Hebrew) meant that a wife in the royal family would have a baby in the usual way. Matthew choose the Greek Old Testament (the Septuagint or the LXX) which speaks of a virgin conceiving, but again in the usual way. God-with-us will have a long echo in the Gospel.

(Vs 24–25)

Joseph is always obedient (and silent) in Matthew 1–2.

Thus we learn that Jesus is descendent of David, he will save the people from their sins and will be God-with-us.

## Pointers for prayer

a) Every family tree contains shadows, shadows which can overshadow later generations. What have you learned about yourself from your family history?

b) In the narrative, Joseph faces a very challenging situation with a combination of kindness and logic, only to have both sent aside by the surprise of God. Have you had that experience too?

c) God-with-us is a powerful expression, inviting me to reflect on my own experience of God with me in my life. Can I name any important moments of God's presence?

d) Every birth is a blessing – even my own! Am I still a blessing to those around me?

## Prayer

*God of Abraham and Sarah, of David and his descendants,*
*unwearied is your love for us and steadfast is your covenant;*
*wonderful beyond words is your gift of the Saviour,*
*born of the Virgin Mary.*

*Count us among the people in whom you delight,*
*and by this nights marriage of earth and heaven draw*
*all generations into the embrace of your love.*

*We ask this through Jesus Christ, your Word made flesh,*
*who lives and reigns with you in the unity of the Holy Spirit,*
*in the splendour of eternal light, God for ever and ever. Amen.*

## 🌿 Second Reading 🌿

**Acts 13:16** So Paul stood up, gestured with his hand and said, 'Men of Israel, and you Gentiles who fear God, listen: [17]The God of this people Israel chose our ancestors and made the people great during their stay as foreigners in the country of Egypt, and with uplifted arm he led them out of it. [18]For a period of about forty years he put up with them in the wilderness. [19]After he had destroyed seven nations in the land of Canaan, he gave his people their land as an inheritance. [20]All this took about four hundred fifty years. After this he gave them judges until the time of Samuel the prophet. [21]Then they asked for a king, and God gave them Saul son of Kish, a man from the tribe of Benjamin, who ruled forty years. [22]After removing him, God raised up David their king. He testified about him: 'I have found David the son of Jesse to be a man after my heart, who will accomplish everything I want him to do.' [23]From the descendants of this man God brought to Israel a Savior, Jesus, just as he promised. [24]Before Jesus arrived, John had proclaimed a baptism for repentance to all the people of Israel. [25]But while John was completing his mission, he said repeatedly, 'What do you think I am? I am not he. But look, one is coming after me. I am not worthy to untie the sandals on his feet!'

## Initial observations

This unexpected and yet appropriate reading from the Acts of the Apostles places both John the Baptist and Jesus in the context of Israelite history. The mention of John at the vigil Mass of Christmas resumes his role in time of Advent and, at the same time, makes a bridge between the time of Advent and the feast of Christmas.

## Kind of writing

Fully fifty percent of the Acts of the Apostles is made up sermons, discourses and letters. For example, speeches are given by Stephen, Cornelius, James, Gamaliel, Demetrius, Tertullus and Festus. In addition, Peter makes eight speeches, while Paul makes no fewer than nine (Acts 13:16–41; 14:15–17; 17:22–31; 20:18–35; 22:1–21; 24:10–21; 26:2–23, 25–27; 27:21–26; 28:17–20). While the speeches and sermons are adapted to the occasion and characters, we are really hearing Luke's theology of history here. In the history writing of the time, it was up to the author to place appropriate speeches on the lips of the protagonists. As this is the very first of Paul's speeches, the first time we hear his 'voice', it is in some way foundational and so especially important.

## Context in the community

There are three large issues at stake here:

a)  John the Baptist was a continued source anxiety even for so late Gospel as Luke's. The evangelist goes to great trouble to 'locate' him in Luke 1–2 and to make sure we see him as the forerunner of Jesus.

b)  The figure of David – a symbol of God's faithful across time to the people of Israel – was important for early Christianity and, evidently, for Jesus himself. Not only are we supposed to recall 2 Samuel 7, but also David was seen as the author of the Psalms. In that capacity, early Christianity saw him as a prophet, foreseeing the time of the Messiah.

c)  The Gospel of Luke and the Acts may have been written at a time when some Christians were rejecting the Jewish roots of the Christian project. Later in the second century, Marcion (a priest in Rome) challenged the use of Old Testament – he may have been the first but he was certainly not the last! The evangelist is very concerned, in both the Gospel and the Acts, to show continuity as a symbol of God's faithfulness through time.

## Related passages

> Brothers, the scripture had to be fulfilled that the Holy Spirit foretold through *David* concerning Judas – who became the guide for those who arrested Jesus – for he was counted as one of us and received a share in this ministry. (Acts 1:16–17)

> But regarding the fact that he has raised Jesus from the dead, never again to be in a state of decay, God has spoken in this way: 'I will give you the holy and trustworthy promises made to *David*.' (Acts 13:34)

> For *David*, after he had served God's purpose in his own generation, died, was buried with his ancestors, and experienced decay, but the one whom God raised up did not experience decay. (Acts 13:36–37)

> The LORD declares to you that he himself will build a dynastic house for you. When the time comes for you to die, I will raise up your descendant, one of your own sons, to succeed you, and I will establish his kingdom. (2 Sam 7:11–12)

> Once and for all I have vowed by my own holiness, I will never deceive *David*. His dynasty will last forever. His throne will endure before me, like the sun, it will remain stable, like the moon, his throne will endure like the skies. (Ps 89:35–37)

## Brief commentary

(V. 16)
Paul addresses two distinct groups: fellow Jews and 'god-fearers', that is, Gentiles attracted to Judaism. Such a group is known from literature and from archaeology and they may have been drawn to Judaism on account of its pure monotheism, high ethics and noble antiquity.

(V. 17)
Paul cannot tell the story of Jesus without reference to the central story of Pentateuch, the Exodus. The use of the third person (they) is revealing about the time of writing.

(Vs 18–21)

These verses are omitted for reasons of brevity but are essential for the coherence of the whole story.

(V. 22)

Paul is made to abbreviate the familiar and wonderful story of the search for a successor to Saul. David is praised extravagantly: *a man after my heart, who will carry out all my wishes.*

(V. 23)

The promise takes us back to 2 Samuel 7 and Psalm 89 (see above).

(V. 24)

This is a summary of both Luke 1–2 and Luke 3:1–17.

(V. 25)

This fits with the way Luke has timed the baptism of Jesus in his Gospel: Luke 3:19–21. It is made clear yet again that John is not the Messiah.

## Pointers for prayer

a) Each of us has a story but it is never just our own. On the contrary, we are part of a stream, a continuity. My story too is embedded in the Christian story, itself embedded in the story of Israel.

b) God wants all of us to be people 'after my heart, who will carry out all my wishes'. What do I do to make my heart transparent to the will of God?

c) The sense of preparation and excitement is tangible as Christmas comes around. What are my hopes this year?

## Prayer

*May we feel this year, O Lord, the passion and longing of John the Baptist and so prepare ourselves to mark the birth of Jesus, son of David, Son of Man, Son of God, who lives and reigns for ever and ever. Amen.*

## 🌿 First Reading 🌿

Isa 62: 1  For the sake of Zion I will not be silent;
      for the sake of Jerusalem I will not be quiet,
  until her vindication shines brightly
      and her deliverance burns like a torch.
  2  Nations will see your vindication,
      and all kings your splendour.
  You will be called by a new name
      that the LORD himself will give you.
  3  You will be a majestic crown in the hand of the LORD,
      a royal turban in the hand of your God.
  4  You will no longer be called Abandoned,
      and your land will no longer be called Desolate.
  Indeed, you will be called My Delight is in Her,
      and your land Married.
  For the LORD will take delight in you,
      and your land will be married to him.
  5  As a young man marries a young woman,
      so your sons will marry you.
  As a bridegroom rejoices over a bride,
      so your God will rejoice over you.

## Initial observations

Our readings open with a passage full of joy and hope, very suitable for the season. It is not quite unfettered happiness but at the same time it is a thrilling passage. The psalm that goes with the reading joins the uplifting vision of Isaiah with more traditional hopes rooted in God's faithfulness to David and his dynasty. The psalm, as a result, rather than the Isaiah reading, sets up the imagery which will be important for both the Acts and Matthew.

## Origin of the reading

Our passage is taken from Third Isaiah and was written most likely in the years after the return from Exile, following the arrival of Cyrus of Persia in 539BC. Hopes were high after the exiles came back but the reconstruction was frustratingly slow. Accordingly, the prophet gives a great message of hope, to encourage the despondent. Some of the pain is found even in this happy poem: forsaken and desolate. It is evident that much remained to be achieved.

The reading is, nevertheless, very fitting for the vigil Mass of Christmas on account of the tone of expectation combined with sheer joy, tipping over into the exuberant.

## Kind of writing

Isaiah 62 is a prayer for the restoration of Jerusalem, which really runs from Isaiah 61:10 until Isaiah 62:12. Our excerpts shows clearly the use of 'twin lines' or parallelism, so much part of the energy and power of biblical poetry.

## Related readings

> Indeed, the LORD will call you back like a wife who has been abandoned and suffers from depression, like a young wife when she has been rejected, says your God. (Isa 54:6)

> The LORD has proclaimed to the end of the earth: Say to daughter Zion, 'See, your salvation comes; his reward is with him, and his recompense before him.' They shall be called, 'The Holy People, The Redeemed of the LORD'; and you shall be called, 'Sought Out, A City Not Forsaken.' (Isa 62:11–12)

## Brief commentary

(V. 1a)
The prophet is unable to keep silent. The parallel lines are uneasily synonymous: Zion is part of Jerusalem; keep silent becomes rest.

(V. 1b)

Note how vindication (God acting justly) and salvation are in parallel. At dawn, the day has broken, but the burning torch suggests it is still night. So, not quite there yet!

(V. 2a)

The parallel lines shift now from vindication to glory, that is, to the public acknowledgement of God's action.

(V. 2b)

In the culture, a change of name is a change of being or relationship ('*nomen omen*'). The parallelism is interrupted to give the origin of the new name: God himself. Cf. 'One will say, "I belong to the LORD," and another will use the name "Jacob". One will write on his hand, "The LORD's," and use the name "Israel"' (Isa 44:5).

(V. 3)

Royal symbolism is used, facilitating the change of focus in the psalm to David.

(V. 4a)

The true feelings and experiences of the listeners come to expression. Cf. 'Zion said, The LORD has abandoned me, the sovereign master has forgotten me' (Isa 49:14). 'Indeed, the LORD will call you back like a wife who has been abandoned and suffers from depression, like a young wife when she has been rejected, says your God' (Isa 54:6).

(V. 4b–c)

V. 4a is turned around and robustly positive language is used. Cf. 'Jerusalem will bring me joy, and my people will bring me happiness. The sound of weeping or cries of sorrow will never be heard in her again' (Isa 65:19). V. 4b is 'activated' so to speak in V. 4c. It is not just a change of name but a change of reality, of being, of heart.

(V. 5a)

The parallelism is evident. Why builder? A more literal translation runs as follows: 'As a youth espouses a maiden, Your sons shall espouse you' (Isa 62:5, Jewish Publication Translation). The word 'son' is related to the word 'to build'. Respecting the parallelism, evidently, the New Jerusalem translates thus: 'Like a young man marrying a virgin, your rebuilder will wed you, and as the bridegroom rejoices in his bride, so will your God rejoice in you' (Isa 62:5 New Jerusalem Bible).

(V. 5b)
This is an uncommon and unexpected metaphor. It reminds one of Psalm 19: 'In the sky he has pitched a tent for the sun. Like a bridegroom it emerges from its chamber; like a strong man it enjoys running its course' (Ps 19:4–5).

## Pointers for prayer

a) We do not often think of God as 'rejoicing', much less rejoicing over us or even over me. We touch the heart of the incarnation: 'Thus we are writing these things so that our joy may be complete' (1 Jn 1:4).

b) Not being able to hold it in was also the experience of Jeremiah. Do I feel any such 'compulsion' to let another into the secret?

## Prayer

*God, truly you rejoice in yourself,*
*in your cosmos and even in each one of us.*
*Teach us to live by such conviction*
*that our faith may be truly alive*
*and that others may be drawn to life abundant.*
*Through Christ our Lord. Amen.*

# Chapter 6

# Christmas Eve Midnight Mass (ABC)

## Thought for the day

The birth of any child is always a source of wonder, when we feel nearer the mystery of life and, in a most natural way, the mystery of God brought near. In the birth of Jesus, we see our God made visible and so are caught up in love of the God we cannot see. The thrilling reality of the Word made flesh is both gift and call. In the words of the first letter of John, 'Beloved, since God loved us so much, we also ought to love one another' (1 Jn 4:11). We are challenged to love the God we cannot see in the neighbour we can see. There can be no separation of these two realities: to love God is to love your neighbour and to love your neighbour is to love God.

## Prayer

*Today love itself became flesh like one of us, so that you, O God,*
*might see and love in us what you see and love in him.*
*May we see you and love you in our brothers and sisters.*
*Through Christ our Lord.*

##  Gospel

**Lk 2:1** In those days a decree went out from Emperor Augustus that all the world should be registered. ²This was the first registration and was taken while Quirinius was governor of Syria. ³All went to their own towns to be registered. ⁴Joseph also went from the town of Nazareth in Galilee to Judea, to the city of David called Bethlehem, because he was descended from the house and family of David. ⁵He went to be registered with Mary, to whom he was engaged and who was expecting a child. ⁶While they were there, the time came for her to deliver her child. ⁷And she gave birth to her firstborn son and wrapped him in bands of cloth, and laid him in a manger, because there was no place for them in the inn.

⁸In that region there were shepherds living in the fields, keeping watch over their flock by night. ⁹Then an angel of the Lord stood before them, and the glory of the Lord shone around them, and they were terrified. ¹⁰But the angel said to them, 'Do not be afraid; for see – I am bringing you good news of great joy for all the people: ¹¹to you is born this day in the city of David a Saviour, who is the Messiah, the Lord. ¹²This will be a sign for you: you will find a child wrapped in bands of cloth and lying in a manger.' ¹³And suddenly there was with the angel a multitude of the heavenly host, praising God and saying, ¹⁴"Glory to God in the highest heaven, and on earth peace among those whom he favours!'

## Initial observations

The birth stories of Jesus are found only in Matthew and Luke, as is well known. Like all Gospel stories, they are written retrospectively in the light of the resurrection. Again, just as in the Prologue of John, they serve to provide a Christological key to the identity of Jesus in the rest of the narrative. Finally, again like the prologue, they establish a significant level of continuity with the revelation to God's first chosen people.

Both Matthew and Luke write in dialogue with patterns and personalities from the Old Testament and, to a high degree, the writing is determined by those earlier models. While there is indeed a historical core (the Holy Family, Nazareth, Bethlehem, Jerusalem, Herod), nevertheless these accounts are 'parabolic' (even haggadic) in nature rather than straight history as we would understand it today.

## Kind of writing

In the context of the culture, this is 'historical' writing, mirroring the conventions and practices of the time. In such cases, the writers use common-places, to express the significance of the person being written about. The goal is to proclaim the present, living Jesus and not merely to present the past.

Two backgrounds needs to be considered, Jewish and Greco-Roman.

### Midrashic Commentary

*Midrashic* commentary was a form of filling in the gaps, answering questions that the Scripture itself did not make clear. Accordingly, we might consider certain of the apocryphal writings under the same rubric.

The Greek works of Philo and Josephus (especially in his *Jewish Antiquities*) also expand the biblical text, fill in gaps, allegorise, and otherwise interpret the Bible in ways reminiscent of the rabbis. Many of the traditions that these Jews quote in their interpretations of Jewish Scripture find parallels in rabbinic *midrash*.

Neither Matthew 1–2 nor Luke 1–2 is strictly *midrash*, however. *Haggadah* was another kind of devotional writing designed to instruct and uplift. The strong links to biblical models and motifs lend a very strong biblical air to the writing.

### Greco-Roman Culture

In Greco-Roman culture, the birth of a ruler is sometimes celebrated with a list of his (future) benefit to all humanity. For example, the Priene Calendar Inscription includes some breath-taking affirmation about Augustus the first emperor:

> Since providence, which has divinely disposed our lives, having employed zeal and ardour, has arranged the most perfect culmination for life by producing Augustus, whom for the benefit of mankind she has filled with excellence, as if she had

granted him as a saviour for us and our descendants, a saviour who brought war to an end and set all things in peaceful order, and since with his appearance, Caesar exceeded the hopes of all those who had received good news before us, not only surpassing those who had been benefactors before him, but not even leaving any hope of surpassing him for those who are to come in the future, and since the beginning of the good news on his account for the world was the birthday of a god …

## Old Testament background

I was nursed with care in swaddling cloths. (Wis 7:4)

An ox recognises its owner, a donkey recognises where its owner puts its food; but Israel does not recognise me, my people do not understand. (Isa 1:3)

As for you, Bethlehem Ephrathah, seemingly insignificant among the clans of Judah – from you a king will emerge who will rule over Israel on my behalf, one whose origins are in the distant past. (Mic 5:2)

For a child has been born to us, a son has been given to us. He shoulders responsibility and is called: Extraordinary Strategist, Mighty God, Everlasting Father, Prince of Peace. (Isa 9:6)

How delightful it is to see approaching over the mountains the feet of a messenger who announces peace, a messenger who brings good news, who announces deliverance, who says to Zion, 'Your God reigns!' (Isa 52:7)

## New Testament foreground

Men of Israel, listen to these words: Jesus the Nazarene, a man clearly attested to you by God with powerful deeds, wonders, and miraculous signs that God performed among you through him, just as you yourselves know– this man, who was handed over by the predetermined plan and foreknowledge of God, you executed by nailing him to a cross at the hands of Gentiles. But God raised him up, having released him from the pains of death, because it was not possible for him to be held in its power. (Acts 2:22–24)

## St Paul

From Paul, a slave of Christ Jesus, called to be an apostle, set apart for the gospel of God. This gospel he promised beforehand through his prophets in the holy scriptures, concerning his Son who was a descendant of David with reference to the flesh, who was appointed the Son-of-God-in-power according to the Holy Spirit by the resurrection from the dead, Jesus Christ our Lord. Through him we have received grace and our apostleship to bring about the obedience of faith among all the Gentiles on behalf of his name. You also are among them, called to belong to Jesus Christ. To all those loved by God in Rome, called to be saints: Grace and peace to you from God our Father and the Lord Jesus Christ! (Rom 1:1–7)

## Brief commentary

(V. 1)
Augustus was the grand-nephew and adopted son of the deified Julius Caesar, and therefore could claim to be a 'son of God', *dei filius*. On his death in AD14, Tiberius became emperor. There was no worldwide census in the time of Augustus. Luke is mixing up a census of Syria, which took place before the death of Archaelaus in AD6, under the governorship of Quirinius. The solemn beginning resembles 3:1. Augustus was regarded as the saviour of the world and the bringer of the *pax romana*. Luke challenges that especially in V. 14.

(V. 2)

Publius Sulpicius Quirinius was a real historical figure, from Lanuvio (Lanuvium) not far from Castelgandolfo, who was made legate of Syria in AD6 with the special task of restructuring Judaea as a Roman province.

(V. 3)

There is no evidence for such a disruptive practice. It does, however, echo the instructions for the Jubilee Year, a theme in Luke 4:16–30.

(V. 4)

City of David would normally be taken to be Jerusalem; here, of course, it refers to Bethlehem.

(V. 5)

This is a quick summary of Luke 1:26–38.

(V. 6)

Cf. Genesis 25:24 and Luke 1:57.

(V. 7)

'Firstborn' meant a particular status in the Jewish Law, without prejudice to other children being born. The old word 'swaddle' is a direct echo of Wisdom 7:4, where the whole context is interesting. Solomon, *son of David*, was also wrapped in swaddling clothes. The reference to the manger was filled out in the iconographic tradition to cause an unkind echo of Isaiah 1:3. It can mean a variety of things: a private home, a room, an inn, a space in a stable.

(V. 8)

The shepherd echoes the Davidic tradition. This has also been used to date the actual birth of Jesus to between March and November, when shepherds would be out in the fields. Shepherds were sometimes considered outcasts. Bethlehem: cf. Micah 4–5, esp. 5:2 (above).

(V. 9)

Glory: cf. Luke 2:9, 14, 32; 4:6; 9:26, 31–32; 12:27; 14:10; 17:18; 19:38; 21:27; 24:26. Shone: cf. the conversion of St Paul in Acts 26:13.

(V. 10)

'Do not be afraid' is a commonplace of angelic appearances and theophanies. The long English expression 'bring good news' is a single verb in Greek, 'I gospel you', so to speak.

(V. 11)

'Today' is a favourite expression of Luke. Cf. Luke 2:11; 4:21; 5:26; 12:28; 13:32–33; 19:5, 9; 22:34, 61; 23:43. Saviour is unexpectedly rare in the Gospels and Acts Mt (0), Mk (0), Lk (2), Jn (1), Acts (2), cf. Lk 1:47; 2:11; Jn 4:42; Acts 5:31; 13:23). Christ the Lord (common in Paul) is rare in the Gospels and Acts, Mt (0), Mk (0), Lk (2), Jn (0), Acts (1).

(V. 12)

Jesus, not Augustus, is the saviour. Cf. Isaiah 9:6 and 52:7.

(V. 13)

Luke regularly underlines the praise of God: Mt (0), Mk (0), Lk (6), Jn (0).

(V. 14)

Glory is the visible manifestation of divine majesty and a strong contrast with the fragility of a new-born baby. Highest heavens, i.e. into the further reaches of heaven, so to speak.

## Pointers for prayer

a) Bring to mind a time when the birth of a child made a huge impact on you. Use the experience to meditate upon the incarnation.

b) There is great joy in the Gospel tonight. Have you ever felt such spontaneous, exultant happiness? A prayer of praise and thanksgiving.

## Prayer

*Good and gracious God, on this holy night you gave us your Son,*
*the Lord of the universe, wrapped in swaddling clothes,*
*the Saviour of all, lying in a manger.*

*On this holy night draw us into the mystery of your love.*
*Join our voices with the heavenly host,*
*that we may sing your glory on high.*

*Give us a place among the shepherds,*
*that we may find the one for whom we have waited,*
*Jesus Christ, your Word made flesh, who lives and reigns with you*
*in the unity of the Holy Spirit, in the splendour of eternal light,*
*God for ever and ever. Amen.*

## Second Reading

**Titus 2:11** For the grace of God has appeared, bringing salvation to all people. [12]It trains us to reject godless ways and worldly desires and to live self-controlled, upright, and godly lives in the present age, [13]as we wait for the happy fulfilment of our hope in the glorious appearing of our great God and Savior, Jesus Christ. [14]He gave himself for us to set us free from every kind of lawlessness and to purify for himself a people who are truly his, who are eager to do good. [15]*So communicate these things with the sort of exhortation or rebuke that carries full authority. Don't let anyone look down on you.*

## Initial observations

Our reading is beautifully laid out and teaches us that, as Christians, we live in the in-between time, our lives marked by memory and hope. It is chosen today because it underlines that salvation is for all, without distinction. The claims about Jesus put the writer on a collision course with the empire (see below).

Many scholars think this letter does not come from the hand of the apostle himself. Titus is a document of the second or even third generation of the Pauline churches.

## Kind of writing

The Pastorals present themselves as personal letters from Paul to significant companions. In reality, they are written to communities (in Asia Minor) to bring Pauline doctrine into a new context. They preserve, however, the letter structure, as in the case of Titus:

| | |
|---|---|
| 1:1–4 | Salutation |
| 1:5–3:11 | Body of the letter |
| 3:12–15 | Travels, greetings, blessing |

The body of the letter:

| | |
|---|---|
| 1:5–9 | Elders |
| 1:10–16 | Warnings |
| 2:1–10 | The Christian household |
| 2:11–15 | *Appearance of Christ* |
| 3:1–11 | To the whole church |

For completeness' sake, V. 15 is added (it does capture the different tone of these documents). Some of the resounding vocabulary used here marks the text as *not* from Paul: to appear; saving (salvation as an adjective); to renounce; worldly; worldly; self-controlled (literally, wisely); godly; manifestation; great; to redeem; of his own; to look down on (all these expressions are never found in the undisputed letters).

## Context in the community

The writer(s) of the Pastorals were facing a variety of threats at the start of the second century. In response, it is true that there is some domestication of the radical Paul but there is more to it than that.

The letters also represent a development of Pauline doctrine in several directions: (a) spirits, angels and the Holy Spirit, (b) the Church as the household of God, with great regard for the inspired Jewish Scriptures. The tension towards the end found in Paul is abandoned – there will still be a second coming, but it is in the very indefinite future.

As for date and place, mostly likely it comes from Asia Minor, around the year AD100.

## Related passages

> But as for you, continue in what you have learned and firmly believed, knowing from whom you learned it, and how from childhood you have known the sacred writings that are able to instruct you for salvation through faith in Christ Jesus. (2 Tim 3:14–15)

> Paul, a servant of God and an apostle of Jesus Christ, for the sake of the faith of God's elect and the knowledge of the truth that is in accordance with godliness, in the hope of eternal life that God, who never lies, promised before the ages began – in due time he revealed his word through the proclamation with which I have been entrusted by the command of God our Saviour, to Titus, my loyal child in the faith we share: Grace and peace from God the Father and Christ Jesus our Saviour. (Titus 1:1–4)

> But when the goodness and loving kindness of God our Saviour appeared, he saved us, not because of any works of righteousness that we had done, but according to his mercy, through the water of rebirth and renewal by the Holy Spirit. This Spirit he poured out on us richly through Jesus Christ our Saviour, so that, having been justified by his grace, we might become heirs according to the hope of eternal life. (Titus 3:4–7)

## Brief commentary

(V. 11)

The grace of God is evidently bringing salvation to all; it is not limited to one people (e.g. the Jews) or to an élite (e.g. Gnostics). At the heart of this first appearance stands the cross and resurrection.

(V. 12)

This pile-up of attitudes teaches us that we are to live truly transformed lives in response to this great grace. The Christmas feast can be cosy and 'harmless'. Taking it earnestly means embarking on a journey of deep change. The Gospel is an all-or-nothing offer of life transformed.

(V. 13)
There will be a second appearance or coming. The Gospel is lived in hope between these events. 'Great God and Saviour' was found in Ephesus in an inscription dedicated to Caesar. For the author of Titus, the Gospel proclaims another great God and saviour, Jesus Christ.

(V. 14)
There are allusions here to the authentic Paul in 1 Thessalonians 2:15–21. The 'for us' indicates that not everyone has responded; it is also an echo of the Suffering Servant theme. The biblical language of chosen people etc. is applied here to the Christian community. Again, a transformed life is indicated.

## Pointers for prayer

a) At Christmas, once we get past the tinsel, we encounter 'the scandalous particularity of the incarnation' at the heart of Christian faith. Who is Jesus in my life? How do I experience his salvation?

b) As we get older, we gradually get used to living in-between birth and death; there is for us another in-between: the fact of Christ and hope we have in him. This is the basis for our transformed living in the present moment.

## Prayer

*Saving, healing God, you reach out to us in Jesus,*
*bringing light into the darkness of human life.*
*Help us put our hands into his hands, that he may bring us to you.*

*Grant this through him, whose light has shone, your Son,*
*our Lord Jesus Christ, who lives and reigns with you*
*in the unity of the Holy Spirit, God, for ever and ever. Amen*

## 🌿 First Reading 🌿

**Isa 9:1** *But there will be no gloom for those who were in anguish. In the former time he brought into contempt the land of Zebulun and the land of Naphtali, but in the latter time he will make glorious the way of the sea, the land beyond the Jordan, Galilee of the nations.*

<sup>2</sup> The people who walked in darkness
    have seen a great light;
    those who lived in a land of deep darkness –
      on them light has shined.
<sup>3</sup> You have multiplied the nation,
    you have increased its joy;
    they rejoice before you
      as with joy at the harvest,
      as people exult when dividing plunder.
<sup>4</sup> For the yoke of their burden,
    and the bar across their shoulders,
    the rod of their oppressor,
    you have broken as on the day of Midian.
<sup>5</sup> For all the boots of the tramping warriors
    and all the garments rolled in blood
    shall be burned as fuel for the fire.
<sup>6</sup> For a child has been born for us,
    a son given to us;
    authority rests upon his shoulders;
    and he is named
      Wonderful Counsellor, Mighty God,
      Everlasting Father, Prince of Peace.
<sup>7</sup> His authority shall grow continually,
    and there shall be endless peace
    for the throne of David and his kingdom.
He will establish and uphold it
    with justice and with righteousness
    from this time onward and forevermore.
The zeal of the LORD of hosts will do this.

## Initial observations

This is an especially appropriate and loved reading for Christmas Midnight Mass and the setting of parts of this text in Handel's Messiah have made it even more familiar and appreciated. The themes of darkness/light, child and the throne of David fit the feast. Nevertheless, it does come from a particular moment in history and has to be read first of all in its religious and political setting.

## Kind of writing

Isaiah 9:2–7 is a prophetic oracle in the form of poetry, reflecting the conventions and techniques of biblical poetry generally. The parallelism is evident, for instance, in V. 2a–b and V. 2c–d. As the verses proceed, there is insistence by sheer force of repetition. Thus in V. 3, we have joy, rejoice, exult. The suggestion of dividing plunder (after and implied victory) at the end of V. 3 is continued in the military metaphors of V. 4 and V. 5. Thus a reversal of a national calamity is envisaged. What has brought this about? The birth of an heir to the family of David. Tremendous hopes are placed on the shoulders of this child. Of course, there is no way of knowing that a child would have been able to achieve all this. Instead, the birth is taken to be a mark of God's continued fidelity to the house of David and the salvation to God will be the work of God himself. In all the colourful imagery in Vs 6–7, important words are profiled: peace, justice, righteousness.

## Origin of the reading

As noted elsewhere, the present Book of Isaiah reflects three distinct periods. The original Isaiah of Jerusalem was active from about 738BC (Isa 6:1) until 701BC, perhaps until 687/6BC, i.e. a considerable ministry of some forty or fifty years. His preaching is preserved in Isaiah 1–39. The period was a time of transition from prosperity and security to insecurity and threat as the Assyrian Empire flexed its muscles. In the time of Isaiah, there were several conflicts with Assyria: 743–738, 735–732 (the Syro–Ephraimite war), 714–705 and finally 703–701.

Our excerpt comes from the period of the Syro–Ephraimite war. During this time, Isaiah preached the uncomfortable view that the Assyrians, under the marvellously named Tiglath-Pileser III, were an instrument of God, sent to punish and to bring Israel back to true faith in YHWH. Isaiah 1–12 deals with the condemnation of Judah (through Assyria) and God's offer of salvation through renewed fidelity. The cycles of promise (Isa 2–4) and threat (Isa 5–11) are interrupted by Isaiah 6:1–9:7, made up of oracles dealing with the Syro–Ephraimite war. This block forms the core of Isaiah 2–12 and provides the theological heart of the chapters. The traditions about Zion and the Davidic monarchy are expounded and explored. The typical pattern is threat, punishment, salvation.

## Old Testament background

Several passages, too long to cite, come to mind: 2 Samuel 7; Isaiah 2:4, 7:14; Isaiah 11:1–2, 8–9.

> He shall judge between the nations, and shall arbitrate for many peoples; they shall beat their swords into plowshares, and their spears into pruning hooks; nation shall not lift up sword against nation, neither shall they learn war any more. (Isa 2:4)

> Therefore the LORD himself will give you a sign. Look, the young woman is with child and shall bear a son, and shall name him Immanuel (Isa 7:14)

> A shoot shall come out from the stump of Jesse, and a branch shall grow out of his roots. The spirit of the LORD shall rest on him, the spirit of wisdom and understanding, the spirit of counsel and might, the spirit of knowledge and the fear of the LORD … The nursing child shall play over the hole of the asp, and the weaned child shall put its hand on the adder's den. They will not hurt or destroy on all my holy mountain; for the earth will be full of the knowledge of the LORD as the waters cover the sea. (Isa 11:1–2, 8–9)

## Brief commentary

(V. 2)

Darkness represents the calamity that has befallen the kingdom of Judah; light is used for deliverance through a new king 'of David's line'.

(V. 3)

God is addressed ('you') and given the credit for the restored community, leading to great rejoicing. A contrast is drawn in which harvest point to the fruits of labour while plunder point to the fruits of conflict already over.

(V. 4)

Note the emphasis: yoke, bar, rod. In Judges 7–8, Gideon's victory over Midian delivered the people from foreign oppression.

(V. 5)

An end to war is pictured here. Cf. 'He shall judge between the nations, and shall arbitrate for many peoples; they shall beat their swords into plowshares, and their spears into pruning hooks; nation shall not lift up sword against nation, neither shall they learn war any more' (Isa 2:4).

(V. 6)

The historical referent is a child born of Davidic ancestry. 'Mighty God' might seem too much for a human being, but the New American Bible translated 'God-hero'. In any case: wisdom, heroism, fatherhood, peace. Prince of peace because the king establishes a safe socio-economic environment for his people.

(V. 7)

Peace is emphasised again. The import of the very last line has been well captured in the New English Translation: *The LORD's intense devotion to his people will accomplish this.* This 'zeal' is a covenant quality of God in relation to Israel.

## Pointers for prayer

a) Recall times when you have 'walked in darkness'. What was it like? What helped you to keep going? Was there a turning point, when darkness turned to light?

b) A birth is always a joy! Think back to the joy of your own parents when you yourself arrived in the world. Use this very natural human happiness to come close to the happiness of today's feast.

c) Endless peace sounds great, but, as we know, peace is always 'under construction', always fragile, always in need of support. Where have you experienced peace? What about your own commitment to be a peacemaker, a bearer of peace to others?

## Prayer

*Loving God, our light and our hope,*
*show yourself once more as our true guide.*
*Teach us to recognise in your Son Jesus the love which you alone give,*
*the peace the world cannot give. Amen.*

# Chapter 7

## Christmas Day Dawn Mass (ABC)

## Thought for the day

Sharing the excitement is a very human response. We have all done it at some stage: some great news in the family, perhaps at a promotion or the discovery of a place of spectacular beauty or some situation has turned around. The desire to let others know tells us that sharing such experiences is itself part of the original delight. Something similar may be said of the sense of discovery and delight we find in the Good News of Jesus. Like, the prophets of old (Jer 6:19) or like St Paul (1 Cor 9:16), we just can't keep it in! We want, we *need* to let others know to complete our delight and our sense of discovery.

## Prayer

*In these days, loving God, give us not only courageous joy but joyful courage to proclaim to others our own delight at the discovery of Good News. May we be bearers of your Word of life to all. Amen.*

##  Gospel

Lk 2:15 When the angels had left them and gone into heaven, the shepherds said to one another, 'Let us go now to Bethlehem and see this thing that has taken place, which the Lord has made known to us.' ¹⁶So they went with haste and found Mary and Joseph, and the child lying in the manger. [17]When they saw this, they made known what had been told them about this child; [18]and all who heard it were amazed at what the shepherds told them. [19]But Mary treasured all these words and pondered them in her heart. [20]The shepherds returned, glorifying and praising God for all they had heard and seen, as it had been told them.

## Initial observations

This reading is simply the continuation of the reading for Midnight Mass. Some of the information given there applies here too, of course. It illustrates a response to the events of salvation and already some are worshipping the baby.

## Kind of writing

### History

In the context of the culture, this is 'historical' writing, mirroring the conventions and practices of the time. In such cases, the writers use standard common places or *topoi* to express the significance of the person being written about. As can be seen in the notes, the history is a bit dodgy and the place given to the miraculous would not count as history today.

### Midrash

Neither Matthew 1–2 nor Luke 1–2 is strictly midrash, a type of rewriting and filling out of biblical narratives found at the time. However, the strong links to biblical models and motifs lend a kind of midrashic air to the writing.

## Old Testament background

### David As Shepherd

When they came, he looked on Eliab and thought, 'Surely the LORD's anointed is now before the LORD.' But the Lord said to Samuel, 'Do not look on his appearance or on the height of his stature, because I have rejected him; for the LORD does not see as mortals see; they look on the outward appearance, but the LORD looks on the heart.' Then Jesse called Abinadab, and made him pass before Samuel. He said, 'Neither has the LORD chosen this one.' Then Jesse made Shammah pass by. And he said, 'Neither has the LORD chosen this one.' Jesse made seven of his sons pass before Samuel, and Samuel said to Jesse, 'The LORD has not chosen any of these.' Samuel said to Jesse, 'Are all your sons here?' And he said, 'There remains yet the youngest, but he is keeping the sheep.' And Samuel said to Jesse, 'Send and bring him; for we will not sit down until he comes here.' He sent and brought him in. Now he was ruddy, and had beautiful eyes, and was handsome. The LORD said, 'Rise and anoint him; for this is the one.' Then Samuel took the horn of oil, and anointed him in the presence of his brothers; and the spirit of the LORD came mightily upon David from that day forward. Samuel then set out and went to Ramah. (1 Sam 16:6–13)

### Davidic Shepherd to Come

I will set up over them one shepherd, my servant David, and he shall feed them: he shall feed them and be their shepherd. (Ezek 34:23)

My servant David shall be king over them; and they shall all have one shepherd. They shall follow my ordinances and be careful to observe my statutes. (Ezek 37:24)

### Bethlehem

Often mentioned in connection with David (1 Sam 17:12, 15; 20:6, 28; 2 Sam 23:14–16; 1 Chr 11:16–18; Lk 2:4; Jn 7:42). A significant echo can also be found in the book of Ruth (Ruth 1:1–2, 19, 22; 2:4; 4:11). The key text, however, is the one cited by Luke:

But you, O Bethlehem of Ephrathah, who are one of the little clans of Judah, from you shall come forth for me one who is to rule in Israel, whose origin is from of old, from ancient days. (Mic 5:2)

## New Testament foreground

The Davidic origin of Jesus is important in the New Testament and present in the earliest texts, such as Romans 1:1–7. In the Gospels, it is important and present even in John's Gospel. David is a consistent subject of reflection also in Luke's second volume. For example:

> The whole assembly kept silence, and listened to Barnabas and Paul as they told of all the signs and wonders that God had done through them among the Gentiles. After they finished speaking, James replied, 'My brothers, listen to me. Simeon has related how God first looked favourably on the Gentiles, to take from among them a people for his name. This agrees with the words of the prophets, as it is written, "After this I will return, and I will rebuild the dwelling of David, which has fallen; from its ruins I will rebuild it, and I will set it up, so that all other peoples may seek the Lord – even all the Gentiles over whom my name has been called. Thus says the Lord, who has been making these things known from long ago."' (Acts 15:12–19)

> And now, friends, I know that you acted in ignorance, as did also your rulers. In this way God fulfilled what he had foretold through all the prophets, that his Messiah would suffer. Repent therefore, and turn to God so that your sins may be wiped out, so that times of refreshing may come from the presence of the Lord, and that he may send the Messiah appointed for you, that is, Jesus, who must remain in heaven until the time of universal restoration that God announced long ago through his holy prophets. (Acts 3:17–21).

## St Paul

Apart from Romans 1:1–7, Paul refers to David as the author of the Psalms.

> So also David speaks of the blessedness of those to whom God reckons righteousness apart from works: 'Blessed are those whose iniquities are forgiven, and whose sins are covered; blessed is the one against whom the Lord will not reckon sin.' (Rom 4:6–8)

## Brief commentary

(V. 15)
Shepherds as such don't really recur in the Gospel. But there is, of course, the parable of the lost sheep in Luke 15:3–7.

(V. 16)
Mary and Joseph were previously mentioned in Luke 1:27.

(V. 17)
The word for what had been told them (*rhēma*) is a feature of Luke and Acts, Mt (5), Mt (2), Lk (19), Jn (12), Acts (14). The range is from 'what was said' to 'an event that can be spoken about'. That is, they bear witness, confirming their experience. Cf. Luke 24:35.

(V. 18)
The 'all' is very important for Matthew and for Luke and on this day means that salvation is offered to all without discrimination or distinction. Here are the occurrences: Mt (129), Mk (68), Lk (158), Jn (65), Acts (171). Cf. 'In the last days it will be, God declares, that I will pour out my Spirit upon all flesh, and your sons and your daughters shall prophesy, and your young men shall see visions, and your old men shall dream dreams' (Acts 2:17). 'Then Peter began to speak to them: "I truly understand that God shows no partiality, but in every nation anyone who fears him and does what is right is acceptable to him. You know the message he sent to the people of Israel, preaching peace by Jesus Christ – he is Lord

of all'" (Acts 10:34–37). Amazement as a reaction is also a feature of Luke and Acts, Mt (7), Mk (4), Lk (13), Jn (6), Acts (5).

(V. 19)

The only two other occurrences of the word 'treasured' illustrate the range of meaning rather well: (i) 'Neither is new wine put into old wineskins; otherwise, the skins burst, and the wine is spilled, and the skins are destroyed; but new wine is put into fresh wineskins, and so both are *preserved*' (Mt 9:17) (ii) 'for Herod feared John, knowing that he was a righteous and holy man, and he *protected* him. When he heard him, he was greatly perplexed; and yet he liked to listen to him' (Mk 6:20).

In the New Testament, the other word 'pondered' is limited to Luke and Acts (Lk 2:19; 14:31; Acts 4:15; 17:18; 18:27; 20:14). The meaning ranges from the literal (to take with) to the metaphorical (to consider, to discuss). Heart also has a certain prominence in Luke and Acts, Mt (16), Mk (11), Lk (22), Jn (7), Acts (20).

(V. 20)

To glorify has a limited frequency in Luke and Acts, but of course it is extensively used in John's Gospel, Mt (4), Mk (1), Lk (9), Jn (23), Acts (5). The Gospel ends with something very like this: 'and they were continually in the temple blessing God' (Lk 24:53). Praising is special to Luke and Acts, Mt (0), Mk (0), Lk (3), Jn (0), Acts (3), even if not that common. 'Seen and heard' make an interesting combination. Cf. 'And he answered them, "Go and tell John what you have seen and heard: the blind receive their sight, the lame walk, the lepers are cleansed, the deaf hear, the dead are raised, the poor have good news brought to them"' (Lk 7:22). 'Then he said, "The God of our ancestors has chosen you to know his will, to see the Righteous One and to hear his own voice; for you will be his witness to all the world of what you have seen and heard. And now why do you delay? Get up, be baptised, and have your sins washed away, calling on his name"' (Acts 22:14–16).

## Pointers for prayer

a) This was no ordinary child. It was the birth of the Son of God. In order to take in the implications of that we can do well to recall Meister Eckhart's reflection and ask ourselves how the birth of Jesus takes place in us: 'What good is it to me if the eternal birth of the divine Son takes place unceasingly but does not take place within myself? And what good is it to me if Mary is full of grace and if I am not also full of grace?'

b) The shepherds were both frightened and thrilled. Good news can sometimes be terrifying. Pregnancy and the birth of a child can give rise to both feelings. Hopefully the joy and wonder at new life outweigh the fear and apprehension. What has been your experience?

## Prayer

*Today, O God of light, your loving kindness dawns,*
*your tender compassion breaks upon us, for in our Saviour,*
*born of human flesh, you reveal your gracious gift of our birth to life eternal.*

*Fill us with the wonder of this holy day: let us treasure in our hearts what*
*we have been told, that our lives may proclaim your great and gentle mercy.*

*We make our prayer through Jesus Christ, your Word made flesh,*
*who lives and reigns with you in the unity of the Holy Spirit,*
*in the splendour of eternal light, for ever and ever. Amen.*

## 🍃 Second Reading 🍃

**Titus 3:3** *For we ourselves were once foolish, disobedient, led astray, slaves to various passions and pleasures, passing our days in malice and envy, despicable, hating one another.* [4]*But when* the goodness and loving kindness (*philanthrōpia*) of God our

Saviour appeared, [5]he saved us, not because of any works of righteousness that we had done, but according to his mercy, through the water of rebirth and renewal by the Holy Spirit. [6]This Spirit he poured out on us richly through Jesus Christ our Saviour, [7]so that, having been justified by his grace, we might become heirs according to the hope of eternal life. 8 *The saying is sure.*

## Initial observations

There are three emphases which make this an attractive reading for Christmas: (i) the loving kindness of God (literally God's *philanthropy*), (ii) all is gift and grace, (iii) through the Holy Spirit we too becomes the sons and daughters of God, coheirs with Christ.

## Kind of writing

The Pastorals present themselves as personal letters from Paul to significant companions. In reality, they are written to communities (in Asia Minor) to bring Pauline doctrine into a later context, responding to new pastoral demands. They preserve, however, the letter structure, as in the case of Titus:

| | |
|---|---|
| 1:1–4 | Salutation |
| 1:5–3:11 | Body of the letter |
| 3:12–15 | Travels, greetings, blessing |

The body of the letter:

| | |
|---|---|
| 1:5–9 | Elders |
| 1:10–16 | Warnings |
| 2:1–10 | The Christian household |
| 2:11–15 | Appearance of Christ |
| 3:1–11 | To the whole Church |

The layout of the final chapter is clear:

Pratical instruction: Vs 1–2

Theological support: Vs 3–8a

Direct encouragement: Vs 8b–11

The omitted verses 3 and 8 of the central section are included for completeness. Our reading is one of the 'faithful' sayings found in the Pastorals: 1 Timothy 1:15; 3:1; 4:9; 2 Timothy 2:11; and here in Titus 3:8.

## Context in the community

The writer(s) of the Pastorals were facing a variety of threats at the start of the second century. In response, it is true that there is some domestication of the radical Paul but there is more to it than that.

The letters also represent a development of Pauline doctrine in several directions: (a) spirits, angels and the Holy Spirit; (b) the church as the household of God, with great regards for the inspired Jewish Scriptures. The tension towards the end found in Paul is abandoned – there will still be a second coming, but it is in the very indefinite future.

As for date and place, mostly likely it comes from Asia Minor, around the year AD 100.

## Related passages

> For the *grace* of *God* has *appeared*, bringing *salvation* to all *people*. (Titus 2:11)

This passage from Ephesians is remarkably similar to our reading:

> All of us once lived among them in the passions of our flesh, following the desires of flesh and senses, and we were by nature children of wrath, like everyone else. But God, who is rich in mercy, out of the great love with which he loved us even when we were dead through our trespasses, made us alive together with Christ – by grace you have been saved – and raised us up with him and seated us with him in the heavenly places in Christ Jesus, so that in the ages to come he might show the immeasurable riches of his grace in kindness toward us in Christ Jesus. (Eph 2:3–7)

> It is not because of your righteousness or the uprightness of your heart that you are going in to occupy their land; but

because of the wickedness of these nations the LORD your God is dispossessing them before you, in order to fulfil the promise that the LORD made on oath to your ancestors, to Abraham, to Isaac, and to Jacob. (Deut 9:5)

## Brief commentary

(V. 4)

The goodness of God is a genuinely Pauline expression (e.g. Rom 2:4; 3:12; 11:22). God's 'philanthropy' is rarer being found only in Acts 28:2. The New Jerusalem Bible gets it right: the kindness and *love* of God our Saviour for *humanity*. To appear and appearance are typical of the vocabulary of later generations. Saviour – oddly rare in the Gospels and in Paul – is also an expression of later Christianity.

(V. 5a)

This verse is perhaps the clearest statement in all the Bible that salvation is wholly the initiative of God. The sentiment is not anti-Jewish because ancient Israelites / Jews were well aware of their status as the *elect* (see Deut 9:5 above). Neither is it a restatement of Paul – who contrasts grace *not with works or righteousness* but with the *ritual law* (dietary laws etc.). Neither is it saying that works don't matter: it is simply affirming that our relationship with God is initiated and sustained by God's grace alone.

(Vs 5b–6)

Christians enter this grace through (a) baptism and the gift of the Spirit (b) renewal (a word confined to Christian usage) and (c) Jesus Christ our Saviour. For this writer, 'Saviour' refers first to God the Father as giver and then to Jesus as the mediator. The Spirit receives less emphasis in the Pastorals, perhaps reflecting the settling down (institutionalisation) of The Way.

(V. 7)

As the final verse in the lectionary excerpt, these words bring out the goal of the coming of Christ: that we might be heirs with him. Two Pauline themes are reflected here: justification by grace and becoming sons and daughters of God.

## Pointers for prayer

a) In the secular celebration of Christmas, the giving of gifts is the defining action. Relationship and love, wonder and gratitude all come into play – and not only in our human interconnectedness but also in God's love affair with humanity.

b) Christmas is a time of rest and refreshment. This is good – and yet, it would be a pity not to rest in God too and experience refreshment in the faith. What shall *I* do to bring that about?

## Prayer

*Abba, father and creator, we stand before you, in awe and thankfulness.*

*As we experience your gracious 'philanthropy', help us to become more and more like you, loving as we have been loved.*
*Thus, may we become every more truly your sons and daughters.*
*Through Christ our Lord. Amen.*

## 🍃 First Reading 🍃

Isa 62:11  Look, the LORD announces to the entire earth:
Say to Daughter Zion,
'Look, your deliverer comes!
Look, his reward is with him
and his reward goes before him!"
<sup>12</sup> They will be called, 'The Holy People,
the Ones Protected by the LORD.'
You will be called, 'Sought After,
City Not Abandoned.'

## Initial observations

The questions being addressed by Third Isaiah have a contemporary ring to them: could they really believe God had forgiven them? In the light of recent experience, could they count on God's continued protection? Who could possibly be the leader of the community? Even more importantly, how could they so live that they might avoid repeating the sins and errors that brought on them the calamity of the exile in Babylon? All this is not so obvious in the short excerpt chosen for the dawn Mass of Christmas day. Nevertheless, V. 11 reflects the idea the salvation is *not yet* a present reality while V.12 expresses the feelings still remembered from the exile – a city *forsaken*.

None of this should take away from the real joy of the reading but just as there is no cheap grace, there is likewise no cheap joy.

## Kind of writing

All of Isaiah 61 is poetry, of course, and these few verses derive their power from the poetry. The typical parallelism is not exact, but the 'uneasy synonymity' (R. Alter) has undoubted energy.

## Origin of the reading

As just noted, this reading comes from Third Isaiah, that is, from the final chapters 56–66. The exiles have returned after the fall of Babylon in 539BC and the victory of Cyrus. However, not all have returned, reconstruction is difficult and there is conflict between two groups in the community. The centrepiece of the writing is chapters 60–62, with five units before (Isa 56:1–8; 56:9–57:3; 57:14–21; 58; 59) and five units after (Isa 63:1–6; 63:7–64:2; 65; 66:1–16; 66:17–24).

## Old Testament background

### Daughter Zion

This term appears twenty-six times in the Old Testament, sometimes in parallel with 'daughter Jerusalem'. It appears in two contexts: disaster and redemption. As an example, reference may be made to the book of Lamentations (Lam 1:6; 2:1, 4, 8, 10, 13, 18; 4:22) and there is a striking example in Jeremiah: 'For I heard a cry as of a woman in labour, anguish as of one bringing forth her first child, the cry of daughter Zion gasping for breath, stretching out her hands, "Woe is me! I am fainting before killers!"' (Jer 4:31).

In these contexts, the language conveys both vulnerability and defilement. In the more positive settings, the language can be quite upbeat. Here is an example, later cited in the New Testament: 'Rejoice greatly, O daughter Zion! Shout aloud, O daughter Jerusalem! Lo, your king comes to you; triumphant and victorious is he, humble and riding on a donkey, on a colt, the foal of a donkey' (Zech 9:9; see Mt 21:5; Jn 12:15)

This refers to a future restoration and the joy that it will bring. The beginnings of such a positive note are found already in Isaiah 52: 'Shake yourself from the dust, rise up, O captive Jerusalem; loose the bonds from your neck, O captive daughter Zion!' (Isa 52:2).

*Marriage Symbolism*

This is an example of marriage symbolism for God's faithfulness to Israel. At this stage, all of Isaiah 62 should really be read.

*Redeemed of the Lord*

In using the expression 'redeemed of the LORD', Third Isaiah picks up a major theme of Deutero-Isaiah 40–55 (Isa 43:1; 44:22–23; 48:20; 52:9). For Second Isaiah, this redemption had already begun in the exile and is to be completed by the return of the deportees. God is also called a redeemer in these passages: Isaiah 41:14; 43:14; 44:6; 47:4; 48:17; 49:7, 26; 54:5, 8). In Third Isaiah, God is called redeemer three times (Isaiah 59:20; 60:16; 63:16).

# Brief commentary

(V. 11)
The word used for proclaim means to cause to hear (cf. the *Shema Yisrael*) and is found frequent in Isaiah 40–66 (Isa 41:22, 26; 42:2, 9; 43:9, 12;

44:8; 45:21; 48:3, 5–6, 20; 52:7; 58:4; 62:11). This proclamation is to the whole world – a little exaggeration in the context – but not untypical of Isaiah 40–66 (Isa 42:10; 43:6; 48:20; 49:6; 62:11). Recompense is a positive statement of the earlier expression: 'Speak tenderly to Jerusalem, and cry to her that she has served her term, that her penalty is paid, that she has received from the LORD's hand double for all her sins.' (Isa 40:2).

(V. 12)

The Holy People: the force of this 'title' becomes apparent when one reads Leviticus 17–26, the so-called Holiness Code. In that portion of the book, Israel is repeatedly called to be holy as YWHW is holy (for example, Lev 19:2; 20:7–8, 26; 21:8, 23; 22:9, 16, 33). This holiness of the people challenges another tradition that would confine holiness to the sanctuary. In this view, the holiness of the people is achieved both through ritual and social practices. One text may serve to illustrate: 'Consecrate yourselves therefore, and be holy; for I am the LORD your God. Keep my statutes, and observe them; I am the LORD; I sanctify you' (Lev 20:7–8). Remote as Leviticus may seem, it is part of the foundation of the Second Vatican Council's teaching on the Church as the people of God. The import of 'sought out' can best be felt by reading Song of Songs 3:1–2, 5:5. The other metaphors – redeemed and not forsaken – were explored a little above. It becomes evident that this apparently slight reading is full of resonance and is really very appropriate for the feast of Christmas.

## Pointers for prayer

a) 'Salvation' is one of those words we use in Church circles. It might be useful to go back to any experience of your own where you felt 'saved'. Examples could be coming through a health crisis, restoring a fractured relationship, emerging from bereavement or depression. These experiences can lead to an understanding of salvation in Christ: freedom from fear of death, purpose in life, forgiveness of sins.

b) When we reflect on the Church, it is good to be reminded that it is first and foremost the people of God, even 'the holy people' of God. Through these difficult times, there is great life and hope in the continued fidelity and extraordinary commitment of the 'ordinary' faithful. Time for prayer of praise and thanks!

## Prayer

*Loving shepherd of the sheep, always seeking the lost and strayed,*
*today, let us hear again your good news of salvation;*
*touch our hearts that we may know afresh your love for us in Jesus Christ,*
*your Son, who lives and reigns with you in the unity of the Holy Spirit,*
*in the splendour of eternal light. God for ever and ever. Amen*

# Chapter 8

## Christmas Day Mass during the day (ABC)

### Thought for the day

There is on-going research into how certain animals manage to communicate, establishing some commonality with human beings. Such investigation makes it clear, however, that language, in its complexity and depth, is distinctively human, a mark of who we are. When we speak, something deeply personal goes out from us, so to speak. Words are personal, mysterious, powerful (cf. *a soft tongue can break a bone*. Proverbs 25:15). God, too, discloses himself: in the 'word' of creation, in the words of the prophets and, now, in the Word made flesh, God's deepest and most personal disclosure. We give thanks for God's 'eloquence' in Jesus of Nazareth, as we mark his birth.

### Prayer

You have spoken, O God, a shattered our deafness and we can hear you in one like ourselves. Let us celebrate the feast, then, in love and great joy.

###  Gospel

**Jn 1:1** In the beginning was the Word, and the Word was with God, and the Word was God. ²He was in the beginning with God. ³All things came into being through him, and without him not one thing came into being. What has come into being ⁴in him was life, and the life was the light of all people. ⁵The light shines in the darkness, and the darkness did not overcome it.

⁶There was a man sent from God, whose name was John. ⁷He came as a witness to testify to the light, so that all might believe through him. ⁸He himself was not the light, but he came to testify to the light. ⁹The true light, which enlightens everyone, was coming into the world.

¹⁰He was in the world, and the world came into being through him; yet the world did not know him. ¹¹He came to what was his own, and his own people did not accept him. ¹²But to all who received him, who believed in his name, he gave power to become children of God, ¹³who were born, not of blood or of the will of the flesh or of the will of man, but of God.

¹⁴And the Word became flesh and lived among us, and we have seen his glory, the glory as of a father's only son, full of grace and truth. ¹⁵(John testified to him and cried out, 'This was he of whom I said, "He who comes after me ranks ahead of me because he was before me."') ¹⁶From his fullness we have all received, grace upon grace. ¹⁷The law indeed was given through Moses; grace and truth came through Jesus Christ. ¹⁸No one has ever seen God. It is God the only Son, who is close to the Father's heart, who has made him known.

## Initial observations

All four Gospels open with a key to understanding Jesus' deep identity before the story of the ministry proper begins. Even Mark 1:1 fulfils this function: 'the beginning of the good news of Jesus Christ, the Son of God'. The writer of the Fourth Gospel takes up the challenge of the word 'beginning' and fills it with deeper meaning for all those born again.

## Kind of writing

These verses adapt an early Jewish Christian hymn to Wisdom, which may have looked something like this:

1   In the beginning was Wisdom
    and Wisdom was with God
    and God (divine) was Wisdom [read: Wisdom was divine]
2   The same (she) was in the beginning with God
3a  All things through her became
4   What became in her was life
    And the life was the light of men
5   And the light in the darkness shines
    And the darkness did not extinguish it
10  In the world she was
    and the world through her became
    And the world did not know her.
11  Unto her own she came,
    And her own did not receive her.
12a But as many as received her,
12b She gave them authority
    children of God to become
14a/b And Wisdom tabernacled among us.

It is likely that the final editor changed the language from 'wisdom' to 'word' and inserted the prose additions putting John the Baptist firmly in his theological place (thus interrupting the poetry). Before that again, someone added elements in Vs 16–18 which have a Pauline feel to them. So, there is quite a bit of history behind the present text. The change from wisdom to word entailed the loss of the feminine imagery, alas. It brought with it the advantage that *logos* serves to unite important themes: creation (by word), prophecy (word), gospel (the word) and incarnation in the person of Jesus (the word made flesh). It mirrors the shift from Jesus in his words proclaiming the kingdom to the early Christians proclaiming Jesus as the Word and as king, God's revelation in a human person.

Scholars have also found a concentric pattern across this carefully constructed text. D gives the benefits of faith in the Word made flesh.

A.   (1–5)    God, creation, humans
B.   (6–8)    John the Baptist
C.   (9–11)   The light; his rejection
D.   (12–13)  Faith in the Word
C'.  (14)     The word; his rejection
B'.  (15)     John the Baptist
A'.  (16–18)  God, creation, humans.

NB: Note the error in the Jerusalem Bible version in the lectionary. In Vs 12–13, 'who *was* born' ought to read 'who *were* born'. The difference is considerable.

## Old Testament background

*Read Proverbs 8:22–31.*

Divine wisdom had long served as one of the most important bridge concepts for a Judaism seeking to present itself intelligibly and appealingly within the context of the wider religious and philosophical thought of the time. Within Judaism itself, Wisdom (along with Spirit and Word) was one important way of speaking of God in his creative, revelatory and redemptive immanence (Proverbs, Sirach, Wisdom, Philo of Alexandria). At the same time, the language was able to negotiate the 'beyond' of God. Judaism's (later) distinctive claim was that this wisdom was now embodied in the Torah (Sir 24:23; Bar 4:1). The language of 'word' (*logos*) was used by the Stoic philosophers to express the presence of God penetrating all that is (cf. Act 17). Both the Hebrew and the Greek traditions were negotiating, so to speak, the transcendence and the immanence of God. Good examples of this kind of writing can be found in Proverbs 8 and Wisdom 7. Genesis 1:1–2:4a is also very much in the mind of the writer.

## New Testament foreground

Here we notice in bullet point form the resonance of this language throughout the Fourth Gospel:

- *New creation* across the Fourth Gospel – beginning, finished, first day of the week (Jn 1; 20; 21). Cf. Genesis 1:1–2:4a.
- *Life* – the Lazarus story – I am the Resurrection and the Life (Jn 11).
- *Light* – the Blind Man – I am the Light of the world (Jn 9).
- *The Baptist* – important early on the Gospel (Jn 1–3).
- *Not know him* – the rejection by most Jews (Jn 5 and 18–19).
- *Children and being born* – Nicodemus (Jn 3).
- *Flesh* – cf. Thomas and Tiberias (Jn 20–21).
- *Glory* – throughout this Gospel, glory and glorification are used to refer to the revelation of God's deep self in the single event of the death and resurrection of Jesus.
- *Father's only Son* – see the long discourses in John 13–17 which express and 'unpack' the relationship.
- *Truth* – Pilate and often elsewhere; I am the truth (Jn 19).
- *'He was before me'* – 'Before Abraham was, I am' (Jn 8:58 – but throughout in the well-known 'I am' pronouncements in this Gospel).
- *Made him known* – revealed through actions and speech, seen especially in the long meditations in the Fourth Gospel (most likely not the words of the historical Jesus, but late first-century meditations).

## St Paul

For it is the God who said, 'Let light shine out of darkness', who has shone in our hearts to give the light of the knowledge of the glory of God in the face of Jesus Christ. (2 Cor 4:6)

## Brief commentary

(V. 1)
The context is the original creation and the new creation in Christ; the Word expresses and articulates the deep being of God.

(V. 2)
The New Testament writers slowly became aware of Jesus' identity with God. This is one of strongest statements.

(V. 3)
Cf. Colossians 1:15–20 and Ephesians 1:3–14.

(V. 4)
The images of light and life recur throughout this Gospel.

(V. 5)
The writer states the victory of Jesus over death before coming to the tragic rejection of the Word by God's first chosen people.

(Vs 6–9)
Anxiety about John makes the writer clarify the relationship with Jesus. This is most likely on account of the continued existence of disciples of John the Baptist, who might claim a certain superiority. Cf. The *Mandaeans* of today.

(Vs 10–11)
Paradoxical and tragic.

(Vs 12–13)
The literary and theological anticipation of the effects of incarnation may be seen here.

(V. 14)
An echo of both wisdom and God's presence (*shekinah*) in the ark of the covenant; at the time, highly paradoxical because of the juxtaposition of word (*logos*) and flesh (*sarx*). Grace and truth equals love and faithfulness, God's covenant qualities in the Old Testament, coming to personal expression in the person of Jesus of Nazareth.

(V. 15)
Prose interruption again to 'locate' John the Baptist.

(V. 16)
God's prodigal gift of love in the Son.

(V. 17)
The contrast of Law and grace sounds Pauline at this point.

(V. 18)
Cf. 1 John 4:12. 'Made him known' literally to relate in detail, to expound or, perhaps, to tell the story.

## Pointers for prayer

a) 'In the beginning' takes me back to my own new creation in Christ – back to significant moments – perhaps even to a single moment which stands out as the beginning of my own belonging in Christ. A prayer of praise.

b) Life – what makes me alive, taking hold of my imagination and energy? How is my life in Christ? Prayer of gratitude.

c) Light – a fabulous imagery. It may be that some particular land or seascape stands out in my memory as having an especially beautiful light. Prayer of enlightenment.

d) The dark side of refusal and rejection – in my life I probably have said both yes and no to grace. Where am I now in my life? Prayer of pilgrimage.

e) Wisdom was God's presence – a feminine presence, because (to use Biblical language) just as a man is 'incomplete' without the love and companionship of a woman, the human person needs to be complemented by God's wisdom.

f) The power of language in my experience as an entry point to appreciating the Word made flesh. What word am I hearing especially today?

## Prayer

*We praise you, gracious God, for the glad tidings of peace,*
*the good news of salvation: your Word became flesh*
*and we have seen his glory.*
*Let the radiance of that glory enlighten the lives*
*of those who celebrate his birth.*

*Reveal to all the world the light no darkness can extinguish,*
*our Lord Jesus Christ, who lives and reigns with you*
*in the unity of the Holy Spirit, in the splendour of eternal light,*
*God for ever and ever. Amen.*

## 🌿 Second Reading 🌿

**Heb 1:1** Long ago God spoke to our ancestors in many and various ways by the prophets, [2]but in these last days he has spoken to us by a Son, whom he appointed heir of all things, through whom he also created the worlds. [3]He is the reflection (*apaūgasma*) of God's glory and the exact imprint (*charactēr*) of God's very being (*hypostāsis*), and he sustains all things by his powerful word. When he had made purification for sins, he sat down at the right hand of the Majesty on high, [4]having become as much superior to angels as the name he has inherited is more excellent than theirs.

[5]For to which of the angels did God ever say, 'You are my Son; today I have begotten you'? Or again, 'I will be his Father, and he will be my Son'? [6]And again, when he brings the firstborn into the world, he says, 'Let all God's angels worship him.'

### Initial observations

The stately opening of Hebrews, sonorous even in English, makes this an ideal reading for Christmas day – poetic, dignified, intriguing.

Even here, however, something of the puzzle of Hebrews come to the fore. Who wrote it? To whom? When? In what circumstances? Much remains speculative, although the implied context can be inferred (see next section). Today, scholars would claim this is not a letter but a homily in which the author wants to show that Jesus' death *both* fulfils *and* abolishes the temple service. This deep understanding of Jesus' death and resurrection is built upon the foundation of Jesus as the final and complete disclosure of God (Son, heir, 'reflection' and 'imprint').

## Kind of writing

This early Christian homily is written in the best Greek of the New Testament, using all the techniques of ancient rhetoric, 'the art of speaking well'. In particular, we note the sustained use of comparison (*synkrisis*): prophets, angels, Moses, Aaron and the temple cult. Our reading is part of the introduction to the opening section, 1:1–4; 1:5–4:13. The four opening verses form an introduction (*exordium*), while Vs 5–6 initiate the first comparison with the angels. As an *exordium*, the opening verses attract the attention and good will of the audience and lay out the themes to be treated in the course of the whole homily.

## Context in the community

A careful reading of the letter allows a tentative reconstruction of the context of writing. (a) The community, after initial conversion and enthusiasm, encountered considerable opposition from the surrounding culture, (b) within the group, some fell away because of the gap between Christian claims and reality, (c) the many exhortations reveal the anxiety of the author that more will fall away, (d) the teaching that 'Jesus can help us because he is like us' reveals the context of suffering and trials and a sense of alienation. The author addresses the context in two ways: theology (really Christology) and much practical exhortation/*paraenesis*. Our verses focus on the Christology of Hebrews.

## Related passages

*Many New Testament passages echo the high Christology of Hebrews.*

All things came into being through him, and without him not one thing came into being. (Jn 1:3)

For from him and through him and to him are all things. To him be the glory forever. Amen. (Rom 11:36)

Indeed, even though there may be so – called gods in heaven or on earth – as in fact there are many gods and many lords – yet for us there is one God, the Father, from whom are all things and for whom we exist, and one Lord, Jesus Christ, through whom are all things and through whom we exist. (1 Cor 8:5–6)

He is the image of the invisible God, the firstborn of all creation; for in him all things in heaven and on earth were created, things visible and invisible, whether thrones or dominions or rulers or powers –all things have been created through him and for him. (Col 1:15–16)

For it is the God who said, 'Let light shine out of darkness, ' who has shone in our hearts to give the light of the knowledge of the glory of God in the face of Jesus Christ. (2 Cor 4:6)

## Brief commentary

(V. 1)
Already the tone of comparison is established, within an affirmation of continuity (*our* ancestors...*but*).

(V. 2)
Notice how comprehensive the claims are: the present (Son), the end / future (heir), the beginning /past (creation). As believers, we become accustomed to such claims but, as Raymond Brown remarked many years ago, these *are* extraordinary claims about a Galilean peasant

prophet who was put to death ignominiously by the Romans.

**(V. 3a)**
The imagery here (given in Greek above) comes not only from the wisdom tradition of the Bible but also from philosophical speculation in the works Philo of Alexandria, for example.

**(V. 3b)**
Thus the writer announces the main argument of Hebrews: Jesus fulfils, transcends and abolishes the temple priesthood. The challenge is acute because the *historical* Jesus was a prophet and a layman, not a priest.

**(V. 4)**
The final sentence of the introduction acts as a bridge to the next section, the comparison with the angels.

**(V. 5)**
The rhetorical questions make use of Psalm 2 found elsewhere (Acts 13:23; Heb 5:5). At the time, Psalm 2 was widely read in a messianic manner.

**(V. 6)**
The verse cited is from the Septuagint of Deuteronomy 32:43: 'Be glad, O nations, with his people, and let all the angels of God prevail (worship, in Hebrews) for him'.

## Pointers for prayer

a) Can I go back to my own times of 'disclosure', when I was aware of God's word to me in a special way?

b) Christians don't just say things *about* Jesus; instead, we encounter him as God's living word in our world. Building on such personal experience, we become more and more aware of the depth and mystery of the identity of Jesus.

# Prayer

*In your words to us, O God, you have disclosed yourself and guided our steps.*
*In the Word made flesh, you have done something even more wonderful:*
*we see the very imprint of your being, as you speak to us*
*from within our fractured humanity.*
*Help us to come to you through Jesus, our Lord and brother who can help us*
*because he is one of us and knows our lives from the inside out. Amen.*

## 🌿 First Reading 🌿

Isa 52:7   How delightful it is to see approaching over the mountains
the feet of a messenger who announces peace,
a messenger who brings good news, who announces deliverance,
who says to Zion, 'Your God reigns!'
8  Listen, your watchmen shout;
in unison they shout for joy,
for they see with their very own eyes
the Lord's return to Zion.
9  In unison give a joyful shout,
O ruins of Jerusalem!
For the Lord consoles his people;
he protects Jerusalem.
10  The Lord reveals his royal power
in the sight of all the nations;
the entire earth sees
our God deliver. (Isa 52:7–10)

## Initial Observations

This reading is very suitable for the third mass of Christmas Day. It has an energetic, uplifting tone and the words touch on the important themes of the feast (peace, good news, salvation, joy, etc.).

## Kind of writing

Once again, this is poetry, showing the usual marks of parallelism. Part of the imagery includes reference to the Holy City (Zion, Jerusalem, sentinels on the look out). We see also the language of proclamation (announces, brings good news), the language of response (sing, joy, singing) and the language of God's gifts (peace, good news, salvation, return, comforted, redeemed, holy arm, salvation of our God). The pleasure of biblical parallelism can be noted here:

> [7]who brings good news, who announces salvation, who says to Zion, 'Your God reigns.' [8]Listen! Your sentinels lift up their voices, together they sing for joy; [9]for the LORD has comforted his people, he has redeemed Jerusalem. (Isa 52:7–9)

It is said once more that God will be returning with them, because in Exile God was with them all along. It shares that vision with Isaiah 40:3–5 (see below). It may well be that the exhilaration found here comes from some who returned early and felt the relief and joy.

## Origin of the reading

As we have seen regularly in Advent, Isaiah is almost a fifth gospel for early Christianity, so widely was it used. It does come from a difficult time, that is, during the Babylonian Exile (587–539BC). The whole section runs from our V. 7 as far as V. 12. It is, in effect, a prophecy of restoration, offering the exiles an ecstatic vision of hope and renewal. It comes as a response to V. 6 just before, which reads: 'Therefore my people shall know my name; therefore in that day they shall know that it is I who speak; here am I' (Isa 52:6).

## Old Testament background

> A voice cries out: 'In the wilderness prepare the way of the LORD, make straight in the desert a highway for our God. Every valley shall be lifted up, and every mountain and hill be made low; the uneven ground shall become level, and the

rough places a plain. Then the glory of the LORD shall be revealed, and all people shall see it together, for the mouth of the LORD has spoken.' (Isa 40:3–5)

Then the watcher called out: 'Upon a watchtower I stand, O LORD, continually by day, and at my post I am stationed throughout the night.' (Isa 21:8)

Lift up your heads, O gates! and be lifted up, O ancient doors! That the King of glory may come in. Who is the King of glory? The LORD, strong and mighty, the LORD, mighty in battle. Lift up your heads, O gates! and be lifted up, O ancient doors! that the King of glory may come in. Who is this King of glory? The LORD of hosts, he is the King of glory. (Ps 24:7–10)

Cf. Psalm 47:1–9.

## Brief commentary

(V. 7)
In a striking rhetorical figure, even the (presumably humble, even pedestrian!) feet of the messengers are praised for their beauty! The message is peace, *shalom*, i.e. a gift of wholeness, affecting the whole person within a network of relationships. It includes the healing of wound of the exile for one and for all.

The imagery echoes that of a victorious monarch returning. 'Bringing good news' is a verb in the Hebrew Bible. The New Testament noun gospel or good news comes precisely from Isaiah. The psalms often speak of universal salvation (Ps 96:10; 97:1; 99:1).

(V. 8)
This verse voices the longing of those in the city who are on the alert for God's return. There is a contrast with Isaiah 21:8, where one sentinel is alone. Here, they are united in their reaction to the 'second exodus' of God's return to Zion.

(V. 9)

This captures the context of the Exile – the ruin of Jerusalem. God comforts by means of redemption or salvation. Poetically, it is the very stones of Jerusalem which cry out.

(V. 10)

The arm is a standard image in the Bible for the power of God and to bare the arm is to let God's power be seen or felt. In the eyes of the poet, this is an international event, taking place in sight of all the nations, all the ends of the earth. See Psalm 98.

## Pointers for prayer

a) To hear good news is a wonderful thing. Go back to some experience of your own which brought you particular delight. When did you first come to appreciate the good news of kingdom of God?

b) Peace is also a wonderful word, particularly in the Bible, where it means health, prosperity, good relationships. Thank God for the well-being you enjoy!

c) The joy which Christmas brings comes to delightful expression in today's first reading. Let the happiness of the feast touch your own heart today, so that you are renewed in Christ and have cause for singing.

d) Salvation for all is the great message of Christmas: this is our God and we extoll him. No one has ever seen God. It is God the only Son, who is close to the Father's heart, who has made him known (Jn 1:18). Let us rejoice and be glad!

## Prayer

*God so close to us that we can hardly believe it, draw us into the circle of your love so that our celebration of the birth of Christ will bring us new life and true joy as we continue on the way of your salvation.*
*Through Christ our Lord. Amen.*

# Chapter 9

## Holy Family (A)

## Thought for the day

Our Gospel today omits – understandably? – the brutal massacre of the innocents. While the story is indeed brutal, it is unfortunately not unrealistic. Its omission is a pity because the tragic side of life is underscored, in different ways, by both Matthew and Luke, in anticipation of the passion. They were not composing sweet scenes for Christmas cards! On the contrary, they were addressing the full human condition, in its mystery, its joys and its tragedies. It is precisely within the family that we encounter death, life, happiness and the sheer wonder of being at all. Today's feast invites us to look unflinchingly at the whole picture, in all its complexity.

## Prayer

God, bless us all as members of our different families. As we thank you for the gift we are to each other, we ask your guidance and grace in all we do. Through Christ our Lord. Amen.

## 🌿 Gospel 🌿

**Mt 2:13** Now after they had left, an angel of the Lord appeared to Joseph in a dream and said, 'Get up, take the child and his mother, and flee to Egypt, and remain there until I tell you; for Herod is about to search for the child, to destroy him.' [14]Then Joseph got up, took the child and his mother by night, and went to Egypt, [15]and remained there until the death of Herod. This was to fulfil what had been spoken by the Lord through the prophet, 'Out of Egypt I have called my son.'

[16]*When Herod saw that he had been tricked by the wise men, he was infuriated, and he sent and killed all the children in and around Bethlehem who were two years old or under, according to the time that he had learned from the wise men.* [17]*Then was fulfilled what had been spoken through the prophet Jeremiah:* [18]*'A voice was heard in Ramah, wailing and loud lamentation, Rachel weeping for her children; she refused to be consoled, because they are no more.'*

[19]When Herod died, an angel of the Lord suddenly appeared in a dream to Joseph in Egypt and said, [20]'Get up, take the child and his mother, and go to the land of Israel, for those who were seeking the child's life are dead.' [21]Then Joseph got up, took the child and his mother, and went to the land of Israel. [22]But when he heard that Archelaus was ruling over Judea in place of his father Herod, he was afraid to go there. And after being warned in a dream, he went away to the district of Galilee. [23]There he made his home in a town called Nazareth, so that what had been spoken through the prophets might be fulfilled, 'He will be called a Nazorean.'

## Initial observations

Our Gospel for today is a combination of real history, typology and theology. To understand the text, it is important to have a clear idea of Matthew's purpose here and his intentions at this point in his Infancy Gospel. The lectionary excerpt omits, for obvious reasons, Vs 16–18, although these are vital to discerning Matthew's purpose.

## Kind of writing

*Typologies*

In Matthew 1–2, the evangelist offers the listeners/readership a deep, virtually complete grasp of the identity of Jesus. To achieve this goal, Matthew makes use of several typologies and a series of fulfilment citations.

The typologies are both innovative and traditional. For instance, the *David typology* is already traditional (see Rom 1:1–7). To move the story on, there is a *Joseph typology* from Genesis 37–50. There we find a Joseph, who dreams, who is exiled, who becomes a source of salvation for his people in Egypt, whose bones are eventually to be brought back. It is not accidental that the New Testament Joseph is named as a descendant of (a later!) Jacob. See below.

The *Exile typology* – emphasised in the genealogy and found also in our Gospel – brings with it a deep note of tragedy, an anticipation of the tragic death of Jesus on the cross.

Finally and perhaps most importantly, the *Moses typology* – richly present throughout this Gospel – is firmly established here as key to the identity and role of Jesus.

*Citations*

The sense of continuity with God's earlier disclosure to the Jewish people is sustained in the series of fulfilment citations from the Hebrew Bible. These citations function as 'static' theological markers, acting as a counterpoint the narrative drive of the typologies.

*Matthew*

Finally, in Matthew 2:1–12, a concentric pattern is clear: magi/Herod/magi. Matthew 2:13–23 exhibits the same triple scheme: Joseph/Herod/Joseph.

## Old Testament background

Apart from the typologies noted above, each citation is significant for Matthew's purpose. A brief comment is attached to each citation.

> When Israel was a young man, I loved him like a son, and I summoned my son out of Egypt. (Hos 11:1)

This text was never read in a messianic way in Judaism. It evokes the Exodus, just as the Baptism will evoke the Red Sea and the temptations will evoke the testing in the wilderness.

> The LORD says, 'A sound is heard in Ramah, a sound of crying in bitter grief. It is the sound of Rachel weeping for her children and refusing to be comforted, because her children are gone.' (Jer 31:15)

In the New Testament, only Matthew explicitly cites Jeremiah: here (Mt 2:18), at the Caesarea Philippi scene (Mt 16:14) and in the Passion Narrative (Mt 27:9). One Jewish tradition located the tomb of Rachel – matriarch of the tribes of Benjamin and Ephraim – at Bethlehem.

The final citation, as is well known, does not exist in the Hebrew Bible or in the Greek Old Testament. Matthew's carefully vague introduction indicates his awareness of this. In a quite modern way, Matthew's 'citation' resonates with a number of significant messianic passages in the following way:

> A shoot will grow out of Jesse's root stock (*nēzer*), a bud will sprout from his roots. (Isa 11:1). ...

> for you shall conceive and bear a son. No razor is to come on his head, for the boy shall be a *nazirite* to God from birth. It is he who shall begin to deliver Israel from the hand of the Philistines. (Judg 13:5; cf. 13:7 and 16:17).

> The blessings of your father are greater than the blessings of the eternal mountains or the desirable things of the age-old hills. They will be on the head of Joseph and on the brow of the prince (*nazir*) of his brothers. (Gen 49:26)

## New Testament foreground

> Matthan the father of Jacob, and *Jacob* the father of *Joseph* the husband of Mary, of whom Jesus was born, who is called the Messiah. (Mt 1:15–16)

## St Paul

> Therefore, since we have such a hope, we behave with great boldness, and not like Moses who used to put a veil over his face to keep the Israelites from staring at the result of the glory that was made ineffective. But their minds were closed. For to this very day, the same veil remains when they hear the old covenant read. It has not been removed because only in Christ is it taken away. But until this very day whenever Moses is read, a veil lies over their minds, but when one turns to the Lord, the veil is removed. (2 Cor 3:12–16)

## Brief commentary

(V. 13)
Fleeing to Egypt in times of crisis or famine was quite usual. The family's sojourn there shows Jesus recapitulating the saving history of the chosen people. Cf. 'When Pharaoh heard about this event, he sought to kill Moses. So Moses fled from Pharaoh and settled in the land of Midian, and he settled by a certain well' (Ex 2:15).

(V. 14)
As always, the obedience of Joseph is silent and absolute, the mirror image of the divine command.

(V. 15)
Herod the Great died in 4BC. Both Matthew and Luke (1:5) time the birth of Jesus to the reign of Herod. The *Anno Domini* calendar was championed by Dionysius Exiguus (c.470 –c.544). The Polish historian Laurentius Suslyga was the first to suggest that Jesus was actually born around or before 4BC, the year of Herod's death. This seems to be right.

**(V. 16)**

Although this action is complete in character for the paranoid Herod, who killed his own sons, there is no historical record nor even any hint of this event elsewhere in the New Testament. Instead, the purpose of the story is, again, a recapitulation, this time of the story of Moses. Cf. 'Then Pharaoh commanded all his people, "All sons that are born you must throw into the river, but all daughters you may let live."' (Ex 1:22).

**(V. 17)**

Matthew is careful *not* to say that the massacre happened *in order that* Scripture might be fulfilled.

**(V. 18)**

This is the third formula citation in Matthew's Infancy Gospel. It reminds us that Jesus – whose name means 'YHWH saves' – came precisely to save humanity from the tragedy of death by means of his own tragic death on the cross.

**(Vs 19–21)**

The Moses typology continues to be quite evident. Cf. 'During that long period of time the king of Egypt died' (Ex 2:23). 'The LORD said to Moses in Midian, "Go back to Egypt, because all the men who were seeking your life are dead." Then Moses took his wife and sons and put them on a donkey and headed back …' (Ex 4:19–20)

**(V. 22)**

Archaelaus took after this father, Herod the Great, but unlike him did not reign long. First of all, Augustus reduced him from being a 'king' to an ethnarch. A successful petition to Caesar against him led to his removal in AD6. Joseph is warned in a dream to take the family to Galilee of the Gentiles (Mt 4:15). It may be that the holy family pictured as displaced persons mirrored the experience of the Matthean community after the Jewish War.

**(V. 23)**

The challenge of this citation was noted above. What is Matthew's purpose here? Jesus was *not* known as Jesus of Bethlehem but as Jesus of

Nazareth. Even more, his followers were called Nazarenes (Acts 24:5). Matthew wants to show that the fact that Jesus came from Nazareth was not an accident but part of the divine plan.

## Pointers for prayer

a) The threat to the child Jesus put Joseph in a situation where he had to make a quick and yet wise decision. Perhaps you have also had to make a speedy response to an unexpected crisis. Who were the 'angels' who guided you to wise decisions? Remember them and give thanks.

b) The whole narrative is designed to bring out the guidance of God's providence for the child Jesus. Have there been times when you have been grateful that things worked out well for you despite adverse circumstances or experiences?

c) External forces forced migration on Joseph and his family, until he came to establish a home in Nazareth. Where have you lived before coming to the place you now call home? How has this journey helped to fashion the person you are now? Perhaps you have a mixture of gratitude and regrets as you look back. Give thanks for the good memories. What helps you to deal with the disappointments and hurts in the past? Bring them to God with a prayer for further healing.

d) The story and today's feast remind us of the importance of the family in nourishing and fostering new life. Recall and give thanks for those in your own childhood who helped you to find your way in life.

## Prayer

*Loving God, guardian of our homes, when you entrusted your Son to the care of Mary and Joseph, you did not spare them the pains that touch the life of every family.*

*Teach us to rely on your word, that in our trials as in our joys we may be clothed in gentleness and patience and united in love.*

*Make us ever thankful for the blessings you give us through Jesus Christ,*
*your Word made flesh, who lives and reigns with you*
*in the unity of the Holy Spirit, in the splendour of eternal light,*
*God for ever and ever. Amen.*

## 🌿 Second Reading 🌿

**Col 3:12** As God's chosen ones, holy and beloved, clothe yourselves with compassion, kindness, humility, meekness, and patience. [13]Bear with one another and, if anyone has a complaint against another, forgive each other; just as the Lord has forgiven you, so you also must forgive. [14]Above all, clothe yourselves with love, which binds everything together in perfect harmony. [15]And let the peace of Christ rule in your hearts, to which indeed you were called in the one body. And be thankful.

[16]Let the word of Christ dwell in you richly; teach and admonish one another in all wisdom; and with gratitude in your hearts sing psalms, hymns, and spiritual songs to God. [17]And whatever you do, in word or deed, do everything in the name of the Lord Jesus, giving thanks to God the Father through him.

[18]*Wives, be subject to your husbands, as is fitting in the Lord.* [19]*Husbands, love your wives and never treat them harshly.*

[20]*Children, obey your parents in everything, for this is your acceptable duty in the Lord.* [21]*Fathers, do not provoke your children, or they may lose heart.*

### Initial observations

In the *Liturgical Calendar*, it is recommended to use the shorter version, Vs 12–17. You can see why once you read Vs 18–19, 20–21, even though these last few lines are the real reason the passage was chosen for the feast. Without mentioning family specifically, the message of harmony and forgiveness would still be of relevance today to any community or family.

## Kind of writing

After an introduction (Col 1:10–14) and a conclusion (Col 4:7–18), the body of the letter has two parts:

| | |
|---|---|
| 1:15–2:23 | *Theology* |
| 3:1–4:4 | *Exhortation* |
| 3:1–4 | Summary |
| 3:5–17 | Old and new life in Christ |
| 3:18–4:1 | The Christian household |
| 4:2–6 | Conclusion and prayer |

## Context in the community

The clue for the occasion of Colossians is provided by Colossians 2:8 and its amplification in Vs 9–23 (too long to cite):

> See to it that no one takes you captive through philosophy and empty deceit, according to human tradition, according to the elemental spirits of the universe, and not according to Christ. (Col 2:8)

From the subsequent verses, it is apparent that this 'heresy' offered a spiritual path to perfection combining in some unclear way visions, angels, feasts, rituals, dietary laws and some kind of asceticism. The writer's assessment is both clear and negative:

> All these regulations refer to things that perish with use; they are simply human commands and teachings. These have indeed an appearance of wisdom in promoting self-imposed piety, humility, and severe treatment of the body, but they are of no value in checking self-indulgence. (Col 2:22–23)

Scholars dispute the authorship, date and location of Colossians. The reasons for the puzzle is that the letter is so close to Philemon and contains much Pauline vocabulary. At the same time, significant teachings are absent (for example, justification) and other teachings are taken to a new level (for instance, the cosmic Christ). There is also a puzzling link with Ephesians, which reads almost as a commentary on Colossians. Archaeologically, near-by Laodicea was destroyed by an earthquake in 60/61AD and immediately rebuilt (at the citizens' own expense, they proudly recalled). Colossae, as far as is known, was also destroyed but was never rebuilt. Bearing in mind differences in vocabulary and unconscious differences in grammatical style (especially conjunctions sand connectives, so frequent in Paul), it seems sensible to affirm the this much: the letter is a product of a post-Pauline school, written after Philemon but before Ephesians. An approximate date would be the 70s or 80s, after both the death of Paul and destruction of Colossae. All would have recognised this document as an updating of the apostle for a later time in the form of a general letter to the Churches in Asia Minor. It may, therefore, be the first of the Deutero-Paulines.

## Related passages

> Do not get drunk with wine, for that is debauchery; but be filled with the Spirit, as you sing psalms and hymns and spiritual songs among yourselves, singing and making melody to the Lord in your hearts, giving thanks to God the Father at all times and for everything in the name of our Lord Jesus Christ. (Eph 5:18–20)

## Brief commentary

(V. 12)
The address is familiar (cf. Rom 8:33; 1 Pet 2:9). Notice the five virtues – great for reflection.

(V. 13)
Reality is recognised: there are tensions and there is need for forgiveness. The motive is clear and comes from the teaching of Jesus (Mt 6:14–15).

(V. 14)
Here the writer is close both to Jesus (Mk 12:28–34) and to Paul (Rom 13:8, 10; Gal 5:14; 1 Cor 13).

(V. 15)
This prayer reminds Christians of the calling in Christ. Thankful in Greek is *eucharistoi*, 'grateful people'. There is a liturgical feel to the letter: 1:3; 1:12, 2:7.

(V. 16)
The first instruction is especially relevant today: the word of Christ, that is the Good News. Mutual teaching and common prayer bring it all together. Thus, taking the Word seriously is very much part of being *eucharistoi*.

(V. 17)
This is a general summary of the widest possible application: *whatever you do*. It echoes a definition of spirituality: what I do to make the Good News come alive in my life (*Nivard Kinsella OCSO*). Practical considerations of family life (not included in the short form) follow.

## Pointers for prayer

a) Do the virtues listed speak to me in my life? It may help to be quite concrete.
b) Where in my life do I need to practice forgiveness and love?
c) How would I describe the place of the Word in my life right now?

## Prayer

*I pray that, according to the riches of his glory, he may grant that you may be strengthened in your inner being with power through his Spirit, and that Christ may dwell in your hearts through faith, as you are being rooted and grounded in love. I pray that you may have the power to comprehend, with all the saints, what is the breadth and length and height and depth, and to know the love of Christ that surpasses knowledge, so that you may be filled with all the fullness of God* (Eph 3:16–19).

## 🌿 First Reading 🌿

**Sir 3:3** Those who honour their father atone for sins, ⁴and those who respect their mother are like those who lay up treasure. ⁵Those who honour their father will have joy in their own children, and when they pray they will be heard. ⁶Those who respect their father will have long life, and those who honour their mother obey the Lord; ⁷they will serve their parents as their masters …

¹⁴For kindness to a father will not be forgotten, and will be credited to you against your sins; ¹⁵in the day of your distress it will be remembered in your favour; like frost in fair weather, your sins will melt away. ¹⁶Whoever forsakes a father is like a blasphemer, and whoever angers a mother is cursed by the Lord. ¹⁷My child, perform your tasks with humility; then you will be loved by those whom God accepts.

### Initial observations

This is a very fitting reading for the feast. In the lectionary, the shortened version is quite coherent and makes sense. However, the omitted verses, while somewhat negative, may reflect reality!

## Kind of writing

Sirach is wisdom instruction, in the form of poetry with plenty of parallelism. In our reading, there isn't much by way of metaphor but there are lots of synonyms for honour and for the marks of old age. V. 15 – not in the lectionary – contains a striking image of frost melting. The full poem runs to sixteen verses, sensibly abbreviated given the quantity of repetition. There seem to be three stanzas: Vs 1–7, 8–11 and 12–16.

## Origin of the reading

Sirach was written originally in Hebrew and then translated into Greek for the benefit of Jews living in Egypt. The book itself tells us about its production and formation. There is a prologue by Ben Sira's grandson, which introduces the whole book. He goes on to say:

> When I came to Egypt in the thirty-eighth year of the reign of Euergetes and stayed for some time, I found opportunity for no little instruction. It seemed highly necessary that I should myself devote some diligence and labor to the translation of this book. During that time I have applied my skill day and night to complete and publish the book for those living abroad who wished to gain learning and are disposed to live according to the law. (Sir 0:25b–35)

At the end of the book, there is an autobiographical poem, in which we read:

> Instruction in understanding and knowledge I have written in this book, Jesus son of Eleazar son of Sirach of Jerusalem, whose mind poured forth wisdom. (Sir 50:27)

The book itself – a late example of biblical Wisdom – may seem conservative. For example, regarding the problem of evil, it knows nothing of the radical perspective of Job and, frankly, it can be misogynist. On the other hand, it does contain a quite remarkable theology of creation and Wisdom. Some of the very best biblical resources for a theology of creation can be found in this book. See for instance Sirach 42:22–43:33. The author's astonishment before creation and the creator is well captured in these words: 'We could say more but could never say enough; let the final word be: 'He is the all' (Sir 43:27). This is risky writing and could sound pantheist but he gets away with it because elsewhere the transcendence of God is so clearly affirmed.

## Old Testament background

> Honour your father and your mother, so that your days may be long in the land that the LORD your God is giving you. (Ex 20:12)

> Honour your father and your mother, as the LORD your God commanded you, so that your days may be long and that it may go well with you in the land that the LORD your God is giving you. (Deut 5:16)

> Whoever curses father or mother shall be put to death. (Ex 21:17)

> Then Tobit called his son Tobias, and when he came to him he said, 'My son, when I die, give me a proper burial. Honour your mother and do not abandon her all the days of her life. Do whatever pleases her, and do not grieve her in anything. Remember her, my son, because she faced many dangers for you while you were in her womb. And when she dies, bury her beside me in the same grave.' (Tob 4:3–4)

> Hear, my child, your father's instruction, and do not reject your mother's teaching; for they are a fair garland for your head, and pendants for your neck. (Prov 1:8–9)

## Brief commentary

(Vs 3–4)

The parallelism is apparent. Cf. 'Lay up your treasure according to the commandments of the Most High, and it will profit you more than gold. Store up almsgiving in your treasury, and it will rescue you from every disaster' (Sir 29:11–12).

(V. 5)

The first part reflects experience: children learn from their parents how to respect parents.

(V. 6)

This echoes the reward attached to honouring parents: 'Honour your father and your mother, so that your days may be long in the land that the LORD your God is giving you' (Ex 20:12; cf. Deut 5:16). There is a related commandment with a not dissimilar reward (an irony not lost on the rabbis): 'If you come on a bird's nest, in any tree or on the ground, with fledglings or eggs, with the mother sitting on the fledglings or on the eggs, you shall not take the mother with the young. Let the mother go, taking only the young for yourself, in order that it may go well with you and you may live long' (Deut 22:6–7).

(V. 14)

The same sentiment is found in V. 3 above.

(V. 15)

V. 15b repeats V. 15a, but with a delightful recollection of the warmth of spring causing frost to melt away.

(V. 16)

This blunt verse echoes an even more blunt text in Exodus: 'Whoever curses father or mother shall be put to death' (Ex 21:17).

## Pointers for prayer

a) Is it true that if people 'honour' a parent, they have joy in their own children? What do you think the link is? What has your own experience been?

b) The verse about the mind failing is, alas, true in the experience of many. It is a challenge to continue to be loving and sensitive, to stay honouring and showing respect. What has your experience been and what did you learn about yourself?

## Prayer

*Great and loving God, you are to us a father and a mother.*
*Help us to continue to love and respect our parents,*
*for in honouring them we honour you,*
*from whom all parenthood takes its name.*
*Through Christ, our Lord. Amen.*

# Chapter 10

## Second Sunday of Christmas (A)

## Thought for the day

We are at the start of the new civil year and beginning again is an invitation to look in two directions. What happened for me in the last year, both in my ordinary life and in my life as a believer, a person of faith? For what do I ask forgiveness? For what do I give thanks? We also look forward and the new beginning gives us a chance to start again on the Way of discipleship. Both thanksgiving and renewal are to be found in today's readings. The Gospel is in invitation to wake up, to keep watch, to live fully the present moment under God, in whom we live and move and have our being.

## Prayer

Wake us up, O God, at the start of a new year and rouse us from the slumber of the everyday that we may recognise you in every moment and in every person every day of our lives. Through Christ our Lord. Amen.

##  Gospel

**Jn 1:1** In the beginning was the Word, and the Word was with God, and the Word was God. ²He was in the beginning with God. ³All things came to be through him, and without him nothing came to be. What came to be ⁴through him was life, and this life was the light of the human race; ⁵the light shines in the darkness, and the darkness has not overcome it. ⁶A man named John was sent from God. ⁷He came for testimony, to testify to the light, so that all might believe through him. ⁸He was not the light, but came to testify to the light. ⁹The true light, which enlightens everyone, was coming into the world.

¹⁰He was in the world, and the world came to be through him, but the world did not know him. ¹¹He came to what was his own, but his own people did not accept him. ¹²But to those who did accept him he gave power to become children of God, to those who believe in his name, ¹³who were born not by natural generation nor by human choice nor by a man's decision but of God.

¹⁴And the Word became flesh and made his dwelling among us, and we saw his glory, the glory as of the Father's only Son, full of grace and truth ¹⁵(John testified to him and cried out, saying, 'This was he of whom I said, "The one who is coming after me ranks ahead of me because he existed before me."') ¹⁶From his fullness we have all received, grace in place of grace, ¹⁷because while the law was given through Moses, grace and truth came through Jesus Christ. ¹⁸No one has ever seen God. The only Son, God, who is at the Father's side, has revealed him.

## Initial observations

The Prologue was already commented on for third Mass of Christmas Day (see notes there). For today, a different translation (New American Bible Revised Edition) and a different commentary will be offered.

## Kind of writing

This is wisdom poetry with prose sections.

## Old Testament background

It would be a great help to look up these passage about 'Lady Wisdom': Job 28; Proverbs 1, 8, 9; Baruch 3:9–4:4; Sirach 24; Wisdom 7:7–9:18.

## New Testament foreground

> We declare to you what was from the beginning, what we have heard, what we have seen with our eyes, what we have looked at and touched with our hands, concerning the word of life – this life was revealed, and we have seen it and testify to it, and declare to you the eternal life that was with the Father and was revealed to us – we declare to you what we have seen and heard so that you also may have fellowship with us; and truly our fellowship is with the Father and with his Son Jesus Christ. We are writing these things so that our joy may be complete. (1 Jn 1:1–4)

> Beloved, do not believe every spirit, but test the spirits to see whether they are from God; for many false prophets have gone out into the world. By this you know the Spirit of God: every spirit that confesses that Jesus Christ has come in the flesh is from God, and every spirit that does not confess Jesus is not from God. And this is the spirit of the antichrist, of which you have heard that it is coming; and now it is already in the world. Little children, you are from God, and have conquered them; for the one who is in you is greater than the one who is in the world. (1 Jn 4:1–4)

## St Paul

> But when the appropriate time had come, God sent out his Son, born of a woman, born under the law, to redeem those who were under the law, so that we may be adopted as sons with full rights. And because you are sons, God sent the Spirit of his Son into our hearts, who calls '*Abba*! Father!' So

you are no longer a slave but a son, and if you are a son, then you are also an heir through God. (Gal 4:4–7)

## Brief commentary

The commentary takes the form of showing where the topics and images occur again throughout the Gospel. Thus, the function of the Prologue as a true introduction becomes clear.

(V. 1)
*New Creation*: 'When Jesus had received the wine, he said, "It is finished." Then he bowed his head and gave up his spirit' (Jn 19:30); 'When he had said this, he breathed on them and said to them, "Receive the Holy Spirit."' (Jn 20:22). Cf. John 20:1.

(V. 2)
*Union with the Father*: 'The Father and I are one' (Jn 10:30); 'So now, Father, glorify me in your own presence with the glory that I had in your presence before the world existed'(Jn 17:5).

(V. 3)
*Through him*: 'No one comes to the Father except through me' (Jn 14:6); 'Indeed, God did not send the Son into the world to condemn the world, but in order that the world might be saved through him' (Jn 3:17).

(V. 4)
*Life and light*: 'I am the way, and the truth, and the life' (Jn 14:6); 'Jesus said to her, "I am the resurrection and the life. Those who believe in me, even though they die, will live, and everyone who lives and believes in me will never die"' (Jn 11:25–26); 'And this is eternal life, that they may know you, the only true God, and Jesus Christ whom you have sent' (Jn 17:3).

(V. 5)
*Light and darkness*: 'And this is the judgment, that the light has come into the world, and people loved darkness rather than light because their deeds were evil' (Jn 3:19); 'Again Jesus spoke to them, saying, "I am the

light of the world. Whoever follows me will never walk in darkness but will have the light of life.'" (Jn 8:12).

(Vs 6–8)
*John the Baptist*: Cf. John 1:19–23.

(V. 9)
*Into the world*: 'When the people saw the sign that he had done, they began to say, "This is indeed the prophet who is to come into the world" (Jn 6:14); 'She said to him, "Yes, Lord, I believe that you are the Messiah, the Son of God, the one coming into the world" (Jn 11:27); 'Pilate asked him, "So you are a king?" Jesus answered, "You say that I am a king. For this I was born, and for this I came into the world, to testify to the truth. Everyone who belongs to the truth listens to my voice"' (Jn 18:37).

(V. 10)
*Did not receive him*: 'This is the Spirit of truth, whom the world cannot receive, because it neither sees him nor knows him. You know him, because he abides with you, and he will be in you' (Jn 14:17).

(V. 11)
*Opposition of his own*: 'The man went away and told the Jews that it was Jesus who had made him well. Therefore the Jews started persecuting Jesus, because he was doing such things on the sabbath' (Jn 5:15–17); 'The Jews then disputed among themselves, saying, "How can this man give us his flesh to eat?"' (Jn 6:52); 'The Jews said to him, "Now we know that you have a demon. Abraham died, and so did the prophets; yet you say, 'Whoever keeps my word will never taste death'"' (Jn 8:52); 'The Jews answered, "It is not for a good work that we are going to stone you, but for blasphemy, because you, though only a human being, are making yourself God"' (Jn 10:33); 'The Jews answered him, "We have a law, and according to that law he ought to die because he has claimed to be the Son of God"' (Jn 19:7).

(V. 12)
*Children of God*: 'He did not say this on his own, but being high priest

that year he prophesied that Jesus was about to die for the nation, and not for the nation only, but to gather into one the dispersed children of God' (Jn 11:51–52); 'While you have the light, believe in the light, so that you may become children of light' (Jn 12:36). Cf. John 21:5.

(V. 13)

*Born of God*: 'Jesus answered him, "Very truly, I tell you, no one can see the kingdom of God without being born from above." Nicodemus said to him, "How can anyone be born after having grown old? Can one enter a second time into the mother's womb and be born?" Jesus answered, "Very truly, I tell you, no one can enter the kingdom of God without being born of water and Spirit. What is born of the flesh is flesh, and what is born of the Spirit is spirit. Do not be astonished that I said to you, 'You must be born from above.' The wind blows where it chooses, and you hear the sound of it, but you do not know where it comes from or where it goes. So it is with everyone who is born of the Spirit"' (Jn 3:3–8). Cf. John 15:4–5.

(V. 14)

*Glory, grace, truth*: 'Father, I desire that those also, whom you have given me, may be with me where I am, to see my glory, which you have given me because you loved me before the foundation of the world' (Jn 17:24); 'From his fullness we have all received, grace upon grace. The law indeed was given through Moses; grace and truth came through Jesus Christ' (Jn 1:16–17); 'But the hour is coming, and is now here, when the true worshipers will worship the Father in spirit and truth, for the Father seeks such as these to worship him. God is spirit, and those who worship him must worship in spirit and truth.' (Jn 4:23–24); 'When the Spirit of truth comes, he will guide you into all the truth; for he will not speak on his own, but will speak whatever he hears, and he will declare to you the things that are to come' (Jn 16:13); 'Pilate asked him, "So you are a king?" Jesus answered, "You say that I am a king. For this I was born, and for this I came into the world, to testify to the truth. Everyone who belongs to the truth listens to my voice." Pilate asked him, "What is truth?"' (Jn 18:37–38).

Dwell: note the Jewish Festival of Booths (*skē*nopē*gia*, matching *eskē*nosen 'dwelt' in V. 14) was near (Jn 7:2).

**(V. 15)**

*He existed before me*: 'This is he of whom I said, "After me comes a man who ranks ahead of me because he was before me"' (Jn 1:30); 'Now a discussion about purification arose between John's disciples and a Jew. They came to John and said to him, "Rabbi, the one who was with you across the Jordan, to whom you testified, here he is baptising, and all are going to him." John answered, "No one can receive anything except what has been given from heaven. You yourselves are my witnesses that I said, 'I am not the Messiah, but I have been sent ahead of him.' He who has the bride is the bridegroom. The friend of the bridegroom, who stands and hears him, rejoices greatly at the bridegroom's voice. For this reason my joy has been fulfilled. He must increase, but I must decrease"' (Jn 3:25–30); Jesus said to them, 'Very truly, I tell you, before Abraham was, I am' (Jn 8:58).

**(V. 16)**

*Fullness*: 'I came that they may have life, and have it abundantly' (Jn 10:10); 'I have said these things to you so that my joy may be in you, and that your joy may be complete' (Jn 15:11); 'But now I am coming to you, and I speak these things in the world so that they may have my joy made complete in themselves' (Jn 17:13).

**(V. 17)**

*Moses*: 'Do not think that I will accuse you before the Father; your accuser is Moses, on whom you have set your hope. If you believed Moses, you would believe me, for he wrote about me' (John 5:45–46); 'Then Jesus said to them, "Very truly, I tell you, it was not Moses who gave you the bread from heaven, but it is my Father who gives you the true bread from heaven"' (Jn 6:32); 'Moses gave you circumcision (it is, of course, not from Moses, but from the patriarchs), and you circumcise a man on the sabbath. If a man receives circumcision on the sabbath in order that the law of Moses may not be broken, are you angry with me because I healed a man's whole body on the sabbath?' (Jn 7:22–23);

'Then they reviled him, saying, "You are his disciple, but we are disciples of Moses. We know that God has spoken to Moses, but as for this man, we do not know where he comes from"' (Jn 9:28–29).

(V. 18)

*Make known*: 'Not that anyone has seen the Father except the one who is from God; he has seen the Father' (Jn 6:46); 'I do not call you servants any longer, because the servant does not know what the master is doing; but I have called you friends, because I have made known to you everything that I have heard from my Father' (Jn 15:15); 'I have made your name known to those whom you gave me from the world. They were yours, and you gave them to me, and they have kept your word' (Jn 17:6); 'I made your name known to them, and I will make it known, so that the love with which you have loved me may be in them, and I in them' (Jn 17:26).

## Pointers for prayer

a) John opens his Gospel with a profound reflection on the meaning of creation, of life and of Jesus. Remember when you had a special awareness of the gift of life that filled you with gratitude to God for creation and the beauty and wonder of the world: 'All things came into being through him and without him not one thing came into being.'

b) We hear the gospel message frequently. Sometimes it goes in one ear and out the other. Then there are occasions when it made us feel more alive, times when it helped us see the way ahead, like a light that shines in the darkness. Recall when the Gospel gave you hope in the midst of anxiety or sadness and helped you to see what action would be most life giving for you and for others

c) Bring to mind people who have had a prophetic voice in the world – speaking the truth for the world to hear, like as a witness to testify to the light. Some of these may have been public figures. Others were ordinary people who have helped you see the 'light' by the witness of their own lives and words.

d) 'No one has ever seen God. It is the only Son of God, who is close to the Father's heart, who has made him known.' Jesus came to us to teach us about God and put a human face on God for us. For the people of his day, and for us, that was a mission of getting us to think again about how we see God and to believe in a God who is a God of love. Recall how the life and ministry of Jesus have changed your picture of God.

## Prayer

*God most high, your only Son embraced the weakness of our flesh*
*to give us the power to become your children;*
*your eternal Word chose to dwell among us,*
*that we might live in your presence.*

*Grant us a spirit of wisdom to know how rich is the glory*
*you have made our own, and how great the hope*
*to which we are called in Jesus Christ, the Word made flesh*
*who lives and reigns with you in the unity of the Holy Spirit*
*in the splendour of eternal light God for ever and ever.*

## 🍃 Second Reading 🍃

**Eph 1:3** Blessed be the God and Father of our Lord Jesus Christ, who has blessed us in Christ with every spiritual blessing in the heavenly places, [4]just as he chose us in Christ before the foundation of the world to be holy and blameless before him in love. [5]He destined us for adoption as his children through Jesus Christ, according to the good pleasure of his will, [6]to the praise of his glorious grace that he freely bestowed on us in the Beloved…

¹⁵I have heard of your faith in the Lord Jesus and your love toward all the saints, and for this reason ¹⁶I do not cease to give thanks for you as I remember you in my prayers. ¹⁷I pray that the God of our Lord Jesus Christ, the Father of glory, may give you a spirit of wisdom and revelation as you come to know him, ¹⁸so that, with the eyes of your heart enlightened, you may know what is the hope to which he has called you, what are the riches of his glorious inheritance among the saints, ¹⁹*and what is the immeasurable greatness of his power for us who believe, according to the working of his great power.*

## Initial observations

This reading offers us another opportunity within the Christmas season to reflect once more on what the birth of Jesus could mean for us today. While both parts of the reading do this, there is a special fervour in the second prayer. The air is invitatory: come and see what the Lord has done…

## Kind of writing

In the genuine letters from Paul, the epistolary format has been adjusted to include a longer thanksgiving for the faith of the recipients. In 2 Corinthians this takes the form of a 'blessing' prayer. In Ephesians, both styles are present.

Vs 3–14 Blessing prayer
Vs 15–23 Thanksgiving report

Our reading takes in excerpts from both. The entire passage should be read; it seems a pity that the lectionary needlessly omits V. 19. Sensibly, the Revised Common Lectionary offers Vs 3–14 as the reading. In contrast to the genuine letters, there is no implied account of what is happening in the community.

## Context in the community

It is not quite sure if this letter should be addressed to the Ephesians, because some important manuscripts lack the expression 'in Ephesus'. It has also proved difficult to establish the context in community which occasioned the writing. Is it to do with the famous and flourishing Artemis cult, or is it to do with proto-gnostic mythologies or perhaps, some combination involving Jewish speculation on the heavenly journey? A clue is provided by the Dead Sea Scrolls, suggesting a Jew with a background in Jewish sectarianism. At the same time, the writing is very polished, so a Jew who enjoyed a good Hellenistic education (not unlike the apostle himself). Perhaps in a context of flourishing Judaism, the writer tries to bolster Christian identity. In any case, the vision is breath-taking, taking us well beyond the limits of the Roman Empire to a global expansion of the Gospel.

## Related passages

> In our prayers for you we always thank God, the Father of our Lord Jesus Christ, for we have heard of your faith in Christ Jesus and of the love that you have for all the saints. (Col 1:3–4)

> When I remember you in my prayers, I always thank my God because I hear of your love for all the saints and your faith toward the Lord Jesus. (Phil 1:4–5)

## Brief commentary

(V. 3)
Praise is the foundational attitude of prayer in the Bible, often taking the form 'blessed be God'. The expression 'every spiritual blessing' is especially rich: in contrast to human givers, God's gift is everything we need. It also places the Ephesians on the same level as the angels. The prayer will go on to describe Jesus in cosmic language; nevertheless, it begins with Jesus the Messiah.

(V. 4)

Christian vocation itself is to be found in the pre-existence of Christ, in whom we were already chosen. The divine will is underlined in Vs 4–5, 9 and 11. The idea that all humanity is in view is also found in the Dead Seas Scrolls. 'In love' will be echoed in the 'beloved' of V. 6.

(Vs 5–6)

Here the writer takes up the Pauline theme of adoption (Rom 8:15–23; Gal 4:4–7). In contrast with Qumran, there is no reference at all to the predestination of the wicked. Predestination texts are also found in Paul: Romans 8:29–30 and 1 Corinthians 2:7. The pronouns are indicative: *he* and *his*. All is centred on God, a highly theocentric presentation of salvation. V. 6 tells us why all this took place: *to the praise of his glorious grace.*

(Vs 15–16)

The reputation of the recipients is not boasting or flattery but a means of evangelisation, leading naturally to thanksgiving. Cf. 1 Thessalonians 1:3–12 and 2 Corinthians 8:1–2.

(V. 17)

The writer moves from thanksgiving report to intercession. God's wisdom was already mentioned: 'In him we have redemption through his blood, the forgiveness of our trespasses, according to the riches of his grace that he lavished on us. With all wisdom and insight he has made known to us the mystery of his will, according to his good pleasure that he set forth in Christ, as a plan for the fullness of time, to gather up all things in him, things in heaven and things on earth' (Eph 1:7–10). The Spirit of wisdom probably ought to have a capital letter, pointing to a more than human wisdom.

(V. 18)

The language here is very close to that of the Essenes: 'May He enlighten your mind with wisdom for living, be gracious to you with the knowledge of eternal things, and lift up His gracious countenance upon you for everlasting peace' (1Qs [The Community Rule] 2:3–4). The eyes of your heart is unparalleled elsewhere but seems to suggest moral conduct. The content of that enlightenment is expanded in terms of Christian hope. Saints means simply fellow Christians, as opposed to angels.

## Pointers for prayer

a) How would my own prayer of blessing unfold? For what would I give thanks from the bottom of my heart?

b) The reputation of any community of faith is important – for the sake of the Gospel. Where does my community stand?

## Prayer

*God of wisdom and light, send your Holy Spirit into our hearts*
*that we may be your children in name and in fact*
*and thereby draw others into the great adventure of faith,*
*hope and love in you. Through Christ our Lord. Amen.*

## 🍃 First Reading 🍃

Sir 24:1  Wisdom praises herself,
and tells of her glory in the midst of her people.

² In the assembly of the Most High she opens her mouth,
and in the presence of his hosts she tells of her glory.

…

⁸ Then the Creator of all things gave me a command,
and my Creator chose the place for my tent.
He said, 'Make your dwelling in Jacob,
and in Israel receive your inheritance.'

⁹ Before the ages, in the beginning, he created me,
and for all the ages I shall not cease to be.

¹⁰ In the holy tent I ministered before him,
and so I was established in Zion.

¹¹ Thus in the beloved city he gave me a resting place,
and in Jerusalem was my domain.

> $^{12}$ I took root in an honoured people,
>    in the portion of the Lord, his heritage.

## Initial observations

Sirach 24 is one of the great texts for the personification of Lady Wisdom.

## Origin of the reading

Sirach is a late Wisdom book, emphasising 'God in everything'. It was written in Hebrew – only partially extant – but it survives in its entirety in Greek.

## Kind of writing

The poem is laid out in three stanzas, with an introduction and a series of conclusions.

| | |
|---|---|
| Vs 1–2 | *Introduction* |
| Vs 3–7 (I) | Pre–existent wisdom |
| Vs 8–12 (II) | *Wisdom dwells in Jerusalem* |
| Vs 13–17 (III) | Horticultural metaphors |
| Vs 18–22 | Viticulture and its fruits |
| Vs 23–29 | Prose reflection |
| Vs 30–34 | The poet's authority |
| Vs 23–34 | These verses help us grasp the writer's goal |

*Prose Reflection*

All this is the book of the covenant of the Most High God, the law that Moses commanded us as an inheritance for the congregations of Jacob. It overflows, like the Pishon, with wisdom, and like the Tigris at the time of the first fruits. It runs over, like the Euphrates, with understanding, and like the Jordan at harvest time. It pours forth instruction like the Nile, like the Gihon at the time of vintage. The first man did not know wisdom fully, nor will the last one fathom her. For her thoughts are more abundant than the sea, and her counsel deeper than the great abyss. (Sir 24:23–29)

*The Poet's Authority*

As for me, I was like a canal from a river, like a water channel into a garden. I said, 'I will water my garden and drench my flower-beds.' And lo, my canal became a river, and my river a sea. I will again make instruction shine forth like the dawn, and I will make it clear from far away. I will again pour out teaching like prophecy, and leave it to all future generations. Observe that I have not laboured for myself alone, but for all who seek wisdom. (Sir 24:30–34)

## Old Testament background

The passage seems to draw upon Proverbs 8, as well as Job 28. For another reflection on Wisdom, see Proverbs 1:20–33.

Wisdom cries out in the street; in the squares she raises her voice. At the busiest corner she cries out; at the entrance of the city gates she speaks: 'How long, O simple ones, will you love being simple? How long will scoffers delight in their scoffing and fools hate knowledge? Give heed to my reproof; I will pour out my thoughts to you; I will make my words known to you. Because I have called and you refused, have stretched out my hand and no one heeded, and because you have ignored all my counsel and would have none of my reproof, I also will laugh at your calamity; I will mock when panic strikes you, when panic strikes you like a storm, and your calamity comes like a whirlwind, when distress and anguish come upon you. Then they will call upon me, but I will not answer; they will seek me diligently, but will not find me. Because they hated knowledge and did not choose the fear of the LORD, would have none of my counsel, and despised all my reproof, therefore they shall eat the fruit of their way and be sated with their own devices. For waywardness kills the simple, and the complacency of fools destroys them; but those who listen to me will be secure and will live at ease, without dread of disaster.' (Prov 1:20–33)

## Brief commentary

Every religion has to 'negotiate' the beyond and the nearness of God, his transcendence and his immanence in technical vocabulary. Judaism achieved this by speaking of Wisdom, from the beyond in God, but present in all that exists.

(V. 1)
Praising yourself might seem strange but such poems are found widely ('aretologies'). 'Her people' will eventually be humanity and not just Israel.

(V. 2)
Initially, we are in the heavenly court, where Wisdom exists already.

(V. 8)
The reading was chosen in part because of the word tent (*skēnē*), also found in John 1:14 above. The language of dwelling etc. is picked up in the Prologue very well. Cf. Proverbs 8:22. For a contrasting understanding: 'Wisdom could not find a place in which she could dwell; but a place was found (for her) in the heavens. Then Wisdom went out to dwell with the children of the people, but she found no dwelling place. (So) Wisdom returned to her place and she settled permanently among the angels' (1 Enoch 42:1–2)

(V. 9)
In other writings, Wisdom seems to pre-exist before creation and even be the very mind of God. In any case, there is something of the divine about her.

(V. 10)
God's presence is recognised in the temple in Jerusalem (a special interest of Sirach).

(V. 11)

Concretely, Wisdom – the *shekinah* ('presence') in the *skēnē* ('tent') – is found in the Holy City, in the Holy of Holies.

(V. 12)

Thus Wisdom is present not only in the temple but also in the Torah. Cf. 'All this is the book of the covenant of the Most High God, the law that Moses commanded us as an inheritance for the congregations of Jacob' (Sir 24:23).

## Pointers for prayer

a) God in all that is: recall your own awareness of how near the Lord is to us all – and give thanks.

b) Recall your own deep moments when the presence of God was somehow 'apparent' to you in his living Word.

## Prayer

*God, closer to us than we are to ourselves and yet*
*always greater than our hearts.*
*Help us to remain in your presence:*
*through your Wisdom in all that is and through Jesus,*
*our wisdom, righteousness, sanctification and redemption.*
*Through the same Christ our Lord. Amen.*

# Chapter 11

## Epiphany of the Lord (A)

## Thought for the day

In our deepest selves, each of us is a mystery: Where do I come from? Where am I going? Why am I here? How should I live? The risk in our present culture is to sleepwalk through life, to be satisfied with a merely material existence. But the human 'project' is much greater. Each of us is really on a pilgrimage, or better on a quest – a quest to become my true self, in the image and likeness of God. My truest self is found by being open to God, in whom we live and move and have our being. By following that star, by listening to our conscience and inner selves, we come home to God.

## Prayer

You are the mystery at the heart all that exists: draw us to yourself, O Lord, that knowing you we find our true selves, and finding our true selves, we may come to know you. Through Christ our Lord. Amen.

## 🌿 Gospel 🌿

**Mt 2:1** In the time of King Herod, after Jesus was born in Bethlehem of Judea, wise men from the East came to Jerusalem, ²asking, 'Where is the child who has been born king of the Jews? For we observed his star at its rising, and have come to pay him homage.' ³When King Herod heard this, he was frightened, and all Jerusalem with him; <sup>4</sup>and calling together all the chief priests and scribes of the people, he inquired of them where the Messiah was to be born. <sup>5</sup>They told him, 'In Bethlehem of Judea; for so it has been written by the prophet:

<sup>6</sup>'And you, Bethlehem, in the land of Judah, are by no means least among the rulers of Judah; for from you shall come a ruler who is to shepherd my people Israel.'

<sup>7</sup>Then Herod secretly called for the wise men and learned from them the exact time when the star had appeared. <sup>8</sup>Then he sent them to Bethlehem, saying, 'Go and search diligently for the child; and when you have found him, bring me word so that I may also go and pay him homage.' <sup>9</sup>When they had heard the king, they set out; and there, ahead of them, went the star that they had seen at its rising, until it stopped over the place where the child was. <sup>10</sup>When they saw that the star had stopped, they were overwhelmed with joy. <sup>11</sup>On entering the house, they saw the child with Mary his mother; and they knelt down and paid him homage. Then, opening their treasure chests, they offered him gifts of gold, frankincense, and myrrh. <sup>12</sup>And having been warned in a dream not to return to Herod, they left for their own country by another road.

## Initial observations

The readings from the Infancy Gospels bear an unusually close link to narratives in the Old Testament. Again, the writer is exploring the identity of Jesus, using citations and re-written narratives. It all may seem strange to us, but the original hearers – Jewish Christians – would have had no trouble picking up the resonances and going straight to the meaning expressed in the stories.

## Kind of writing

This is a kind of *haggadah*, a Rabbinic style of writing which explores and exposes meaning by a resonant acoustic of echoes, thereby creating devotional and uplifting literature. Everything is in some way symbolic, the star, the magi, the king, Bethlehem and the gifts, pointing to the identity of Jesus and the inclusion of the Gentiles in salvation.

# Old Testament background

### Balaam

Behind the story of the magi – wise men – lies the story of Balaam from Numbers 22–24. In the Book of Numbers, an evil king of Moab tries to use the seer/magus Balaam to bring disaster on the people of Israel 'because they were so numerous'. Against God's will, Balaam obeys the king, but at the point of cursing Israel, Balaam utters an oracle of future hope. This oracle was read in later times as a Messianic promise.

'I see him, but not now; I behold him, but not near – a star shall come out of Jacob, and a sceptre shall rise out of Israel' (Num 24:17).

The author takes from this story the narrative of an evil King (Balak / Herod), trying to bring disaster (on Israel / on the Messiah), by means of Balaam (a seer / the Magi). The star in the story comes from Numbers 24:17 above and alerts the reader this time to Messianic fulfilment.

### Gifts of the Magi

The gifts offered by the magi call to mind a universalist text in Isaiah: 'A multitude of camels shall cover you, the young camels of Midian and Ephah; all those from Sheba shall come. They shall bring gold and frankincense, and shall proclaim the praise of the LORD' (Isa 60:6).

It was concluded from this text as well that the mode of transport of the magi was camels, although Matthew supplies no such detail.

### Gentiles

The Magi as a symbol of the Gentiles comes from an echo in Psalm 72: 'May the kings of Tarshish and of the isles render him tribute, may the kings of Sheba and Seba bring gifts. May all kings fall down before him, all nations give him service' (Ps 72:10–11).

*Bethlehem*

Bethlehem, the city of David, is mentioned frequently in the Old Testament, unlike Nazareth. The proof text provided was, at the time, read as a messianic prophecy: 'But you, O Bethlehem of Ephrathah, who are one of the little clans of Judah, from you shall come forth for me one who is to rule in Israel, whose origin is from of old, from ancient days' (Mic 5:2).

## New Testament foreground

*Jesus and the Gentiles*

Matthew's Gospel reflects the historical memory that Jesus did not himself directly evangelise the Gentiles, at least initially: 'These twelve Jesus sent out with the following instructions: "Go nowhere among the Gentiles, and enter no town of the Samaritans, but go rather to the lost sheep of the house of Israel"' (Mt 10:5–7).

Nevertheless, in Matthew's Gospel and community, the Gentiles are an important audience of the Good News, Mt (15), Mk (6), Lk (13), Jn (5).

At the start of the ministry –

> Now when Jesus heard that John had been arrested, he withdrew to Galilee. He left Nazareth and made his home in Capernaum by the sea, in the territory of Zebulun and Naphtali, so that what had been spoken through the prophet Isaiah might be fulfilled: 'Land of Zebulun, land of Naphtali, on the road by the sea, across the Jordan, Galilee of the Gentiles – the people who sat in darkness have seen a great light, and for those who sat in the region and shadow of death light has dawned.' From that time Jesus began to proclaim, 'Repent, for the kingdom of heaven has come near.' (Mt 4:12–17)

During the ministry –

> When Jesus became aware of this, he departed. Many crowds followed him, and he cured all of them, and he ordered them not to make him known. This was to fulfil what had been spoken through the prophet Isaiah: 'Here is my servant, whom I have chosen, my beloved, with whom my soul is well pleased. I will put my Spirit upon him, and he will proclaim justice to the Gentiles. He will not wrangle or cry aloud, nor will anyone hear his voice in the streets. He will not break a bruised reed or quench a smouldering wick until he brings justice to victory. And in his name the Gentiles will hope.' (Mt 12:15–21)

At the close of the Gospel –

> Now the eleven disciples went to Galilee, to the mountain to which Jesus had directed them. When they saw him, they worshiped him; but some doubted. And Jesus came and said to them, 'All authority in heaven and on earth has been given to me. Go therefore and make disciples of all nations, baptising them in the name of the Father and of the Son and of the Holy Spirit, and teaching them to obey everything that I have commanded you. And remember, I am with you always, to the end of the age.' (Mt 28:16–20)

St Paul

> Now to God who is able to strengthen you according to my gospel and the proclamation of Jesus Christ, according to the revelation of the mystery that was kept secret for long ages but is now disclosed, and through the prophetic writings is made known to all the Gentiles, according to the command of the eternal God, to bring about the obedience of faith – to the only wise God, through Jesus Christ, to whom be the glory forever! Amen. (Rom 16:25–27)

## Brief commentary

Once the Old Testament correspondences and the Gospel anticipations have been uncovered the text practically comments itself. Nevertheless:

(V. 1)

This is King Herod the Great, who died in 4BC. The 'wise men' are literally 'magi'. Magus, a Persian loan word, covers a range of meanings: wise man and priest, who was expert in astrology, interpretation of dreams and various other occult arts. From the East: traditionally, the source of wisdom.

(V. 2)

The Gentiles identify universal hope in the Jewish Messiah and king.

(V. 3)

The historical Herod was quite paranoid about usurpers and even had some of his sons killed. Augustus said of him: 'I would prefer to be his pig [*hus*] than his son [*huios*]'. This was after Herod put his two favourite sons, Aristobolus and Alexander, to death (he had already executed their mother, his favourite wife Mariamne). He was an exceptionally unstable, not to stay murderous, spouse and parent.

(V. 5)

Matthew has Bible experts (like himself) identify the birth-place of the Messiah, with a proof-text from Micah. 'Shepherd' reminds us of David, the great symbol of God's faithfulness through time.

(V. 7)

The (f)rank hypocrisy of Herod links this symbolic tale with the massacre of the innocents to follow.

(V. 10)

Joy comes back in Matthew 28:8 at the empty tomb. For other uses, see Matthew 2:10; 13:20, 44; 25:21, 23; 28:8.

(V. 11)

Fulfilling Psalm 72 and Isaiah 60, as noted above.

(V. 12)

With no further narrative use for them, the Magi are taken 'off stage ' somewhat peremptorily.

## Pointers for prayer

a) What is the star (the vision, hope or purpose) which lights up your journey?

b) Like the wise men, our life journey is not one we travel alone. Who are the people who share you life journey now?

c) The wise men travelled bearing gifts. What gift do you bring with you on the journey?

d) At times the wise men lost sight of the star. What clouds have obscured your star?

e) Who, or what, might be Herod for you now? What forces, within or without, could subvert the dream or goal?

## Prayer

*Lord God of the nations, we have seen the*
*star of your glory rising in splendour.*
*The radiance of your incarnate Word pierces the darkness*
*that covers the earth and signals the dawn of peace and justice.*

*Make radiant the lives of your people with that same brightness,*
*and beckon all the nations to walk as one in your light.*

*We ask this through Jesus Christ, your Word made flesh,*
*who lives and reigns with you in the unity of the Holy Spirit,*
*in the splendour of eternal light, God for ever and ever. Amen.*

## 🌿 Second Reading 🌿

**Eph 2:1** *This is the reason that I Paul am a prisoner for Christ Jesus for the sake of you Gentiles –* ²for surely you have already heard of the commission of God's grace that was given me for you, ³and how the mystery was made known to me by revelation, as I wrote above in a few words, ⁴*a reading of which will enable you to perceive my understanding of the mystery of Christ.* ⁵In former generations this mystery was not made known to humankind, as it has now been revealed to his holy apostles and prophets by the Spirit: ⁶that is, the Gentiles have become fellow heirs, members of the same body, and sharers in the promise in Christ Jesus through the gospel.

## Initial observations

In liturgical tradition, the epiphany embraces no fewer than three Gospel stories: the Magi, the Baptism and the Wedding Feast at Cana. Each of these is a kind disclosure or revelation. The feast, then celebrates something 'being made known' or revealed and the reading from Ephesians is thus especially fitting.

## Kind of writing

It can be tricky to follow the sequence of prayer and digression in Ephesians. In the view of many, Ephesians 3:2–13 forms a digression on the origin of Paul's gospel and apostleship. That is apparent from the abruptness of V. 2. V. 1 itself is an attempt to pick up a much earlier intercession from Ephesians 1:16–19. But then Ephesians 3:1 is itself then subject to a digression, and the prayer will be completed only in Ephesians 3:14–19. It may help to see recomposed sequence as follows:

I do not cease to give thanks for you as I remember you in my prayers. I pray that the God of our Lord Jesus Christ, the Father of glory, may give you a spirit of wisdom and revelation as you come to know him, so that, with the eyes of your heart enlightened, you may know what is the hope to which he has called you, what are the riches of his glorious inheritance among the saints, and what is the immeasurable greatness of his power for us who believe, according to the working of his great power. (Eph 1:16–19)

This is the reason that I Paul am a prisoner for Christ Jesus for the sake of you Gentiles. (Eph 3:1)

For this reason I bow my knees before the Father, from whom every family in heaven and on earth takes its name. I pray that, according to the riches of his glory, he may grant that you may be strengthened in your inner being with power through his Spirit, and that Christ may dwell in your hearts through faith, as you are being rooted and grounded in love. I pray that you may have the power to comprehend, with all the saints, what is the breadth and length and height and depth, and to know the love of Christ that surpasses knowledge, so that you may be filled with all the fullness of God. (Eph 3:14–19)

## Context in the community

As noted elsewhere, there is a discussion about the Pauline authorship of this letter. A common solution is that the text was written by a disciple of Paul, after the apostle's death, to bring his teaching to bear in new and later contexts. The reasons for doubting Pauline authorship include the vocabulary, the theology and the unusual relationship with Colossians.

## Related passages

But now in Christ Jesus you who once were far off have been brought near by the blood of Christ. For he is our peace; in his flesh he has made both groups into one and has broken down the dividing wall, that is, the hostility between us. He has abolished the law with its commandments and ordinances, that he might create in himself one new humanity in place of the two, thus making peace, and might reconcile both groups to God in one body through the cross, thus putting to death that hostility through it. So he came and proclaimed peace to you who were far off and peace to those who were near; for through him both of us have access in one Spirit to the Father. (Eph 2:13–18)

## Brief commentary

(V. 1)
The writer begins a prayer but it continues with the same words form V. 14 onwards.

(V. 2)
The word commission can be found also here: 'as a *plan* for the fullness of time, to gather up all things in him, things in heaven and things on earth' (Eph 1:10); 'and to make everyone see what is the plan of the mystery hidden for ages in God who created all things' (Eph 3:9). Thus, Paul's ministry is part of a wider commission or plan. This commission was given *to* Paul *for* others. It is presumed the hearers are familiar with Paul.

(V. 3)
Mystery is used in different sense across the Pauline corpus and is evidently more common in the deutero–pauline letters: Romans 11:25; 16:25; 1 Corinthians 2:1, 7; 4:1; 13:2; 14:2; 15:51; Ephesians 1:9; 3:3–4, 9; 5:32; 6:19; Colossians 1:26–27; 2:2; 4:3; 2 Thessalonians 2:7; 1 Timothy 3:9, 16. It refers to the unity of Jews and Gentiles in the one people of God, already firmly established by the time of writing. See the important Ephesians 2:13–18 above. For revelation see Galatians 1:11–12, 15–16. Daniel 2 is also part of the background.

(V. 4)
Omitted in the lectionary for the sake of clarity, this verse sends the hearers back to the whole Pauline mission and theology. This grasp of

God's plan, entrusted to an individual, is then discerned and appropriated by the Church as whole.

**(V. 5)**

This amounts to a denial of a pattern found widely in the New Testament and in Paul, that is, that the Scripture *foretell* and Christians then *confirm*. For our author, the revelation is new and made through the spiritual agents of the Christian community. Cf. 'I became its servant according to God's commission that was given to me for you, to make the word of God fully known, the mystery that has been hidden throughout the ages and generations but has now been revealed to his saints' (Col 1:25–26).

**(V. 6)**

This verse compresses what has been said more fully in Ephesians 2:13–18. Note the vocabulary of heirs, body, promise and gospel, all genuine Pauline expressions. Cf. Ephesians 2:19. 'In' means 'by means of', an instrumental use.

## Pointers for prayer

Disclosure and wonder are both present, inviting reflection on my own moments of revelation and awe.

## Prayer

*O the depth of the riches and wisdom and knowledge of God!*
*How unsearchable are his judgments and how inscrutable his ways!*

*'For who has known the mind of the Lord? Or who has been his counsellor?'*

*'Or who has given a gift to him, to receive a gift in return?'*
*For from him and through him and to him are all things.*
*To him be the glory forever. Amen.*

(Rom 11:33–36)

## 🌿 First Reading 🌿

**Isa 60:1** 'Arise! Shine! For your light arrives!
   The splendour of the LORD shines on you!
² For, look, darkness covers the earth
   and deep darkness covers the nations,
but the LORD shines on you;
   his splendour appears over you.
³ Nations come to your light,
   kings to your bright light.
⁴ Look all around you!
   They all gather and come to you–
your sons come from far away
   and your daughters are escorted by guardians.
⁵ Then you will look and smile,
   you will be excited and your heart will swell with pride.
For the riches of distant lands will belong to you
   and the wealth of nations will come to you.
⁶ Camel caravans will cover your roads,
   young camels from Midian and Ephah.
All the merchants of Sheba will come,
   bringing gold and incense
   and singing praises to the LORD.

## Initial observations

As even a cursory glance will reveal, the reading is extremely well chosen. Firstly, because of the symbolism of light (more below). Secondly, because of the gathering / coming together of all the faithful. Following a very early intuition based on this text and Psalm 72, the reading adds pictorially both the *royal* status of the Magi and their mode of *transport*. The mention of gold and frankincense probably inspired the imaginative filling in of these details. Notice also that *three* places are mentioned.

## Kind of writing

The writing is poetry and in this case it is almost a textbook example of 'parallelism' whereby the second line repeats the first, but in more concrete, sometimes more elaborate vocabulary. For example, V. 1 and 2 or V. 5.

Our excerpt comes from a longer section (Isa 60:1–62:12) and even within that the subsection Isaiah 60:1–22 offers a poem on the light of the Lord. This is in response to Isaiah 59:9–10, which reads: 'Therefore justice is far from us, and righteousness does not reach us; we wait for light, and lo! there is darkness; and for brightness, but we walk in gloom. We grope like the blind along a wall, groping like those who have no eyes; we stumble at noon as in the twilight, among the vigorous as though we were dead.'

## Origin of the reading

Isaiah 60 comes from Third Isaiah, a prophet or prophets writing in the tradition of Isaiah of Jerusalem, but reflecting a much later situation after the return from the exile in Babylon.

## Old Testament background

Then your light shall break forth like the dawn, and your healing shall spring up quickly; your vindicator shall go before you, the glory of the LORD shall be your rear guard. (Isa 58:8)

… if you offer your food to the hungry and satisfy the needs of the afflicted, then your light shall rise in the darkness and your gloom be like the noonday. (Isa 58:10)

Therefore justice is far from us, and righteousness does not reach us; we wait for light, and lo! there is darkness; and for brightness, but we walk in gloom. (Isa 59:9)

The sun shall no longer be your light by day, nor for brightness shall the moon give light to you by night; but the LORD will be your everlasting light, and your God will be your glory. Your sun shall no more go down, or your moon withdraw itself; for the LORD will be your everlasting light, and your days of mourning shall be ended. (Isa 60:19–20)

## Brief commentary

To illustrate the theological integrity of this composite book, it may be sufficient to observe that there are many echoes, in the whole of Isaiah 60:1–22, of earlier passages in Isaiah.

(V. 1)
This text presumes that the temple has been rebuilt and that all peoples will comes there to worship. Here it is no longer God who will be their light: they themselves are light and they should shine. Cf. Matthew 5:14–15.

(V. 2)
After 2a, the repetition in 2b refers the shadow of death or deadly darkness. The Lord's glory is not so much his splendour as the full presence of God.

(V. 3)
Notice the delightful evolution of the poetry: not just nations but also kings; not just light but also the brightness of your dawn.

(V. 4)
Cf. Isaiah 40:10–11. At this point, the addressees seem to be at home in Jerusalem, perhaps in the Temple. Very young children are envisaged.

(V. 5)
V. 5a–b expresses the spontaneous joy, even exhilaration, at the prospect of salvation. V. 5c–d might seem rather greedy, but it is an echo from the book of Exodus, reflecting the despoilment of the Egyptians before departure (Ex 12:13–36). In any case, the bringing of gifts fits the feast. Midian is associated with the Gulf of Aqaba, as is Ephah. Sheba

is in south west of (modern) Arabia. In any case, a substantial distance is imagined.

(V. 6)

Cf. Isaiah 40:5. This is where we get the idea that camels are part of the story! The gold and frankincense of V. 6c are intended for worship, as V. 6d makes clear. Frankincense is a resin, mentioned in both the Old Testament and New Testament as a highly desired and esteemed product. The trade collapsed in the fifth century AD, after the Moslems forbade its use at funerals.

## Pointers for prayer

a) Although the passage is indeed about light, it does acknowledge the need of light as we experience darkness. Not only do we need light, we are to be light as Matthew 5 puts it.

b) The reading is exuberant, to a degree we might find hard to rise to, and yet, joy is truly part of our faith experience.

c) It all culminates in praise of the Lord, that spontaneous gratitude towards God who has loved us so much as to be one of us, the great mystery of Christmas.

d) The sense of pilgrimage, homecoming is very much part of the reading and, of course, part of Christian imagination. Think only of *Pilgrim's Progress*. Reflect on your one journey of faith, until today.

## Prayer

*We praise you, God, for the gift of light in creation,*
*sunlight and moonlight, illuminating all you have made.*

*Above all we thank you for the light of Christ, that you have shone in our*
*hearts. May we welcome this light and became bearers of you light to all*
*around us. Through Christ our Lord. Amen.*

# Chapter 12

## Baptism of the Lord (A)

## Thought for the day

Begin by recalling some special moment between yourself and your parents. Did you ever hear from them the equivalent of 'This is (or 'you are') my son, my daughter, the beloved: my favour rests on you'? In Jesus' ministry, on several occasions, he felt such a word from his Abba, his Father. His baptism by John was one such moment, as was the Transfiguration later on. Such deep love and affirmation grounded him as a human being and as God's prophet to the people of Israel. Our sense of calling grows out of our relationship with the Father, whose beloved we are, whose favour we too enjoy.

## Prayer

*Let us hear again, Abba, Father, your words of favour to each one of us.*
*Direct us on the Way of discipleship,*
*that we may be bearers of the Good News*
*by simply being who we truly are before you, your children.*
*Through Christ our Lord. Amen.*

##  Gospel

**Mt 3:13** Then Jesus came from Galilee to John at the Jordan, to be baptised by him. [14]John would have prevented him, saying, 'I need to be baptised by you, and do you come to me?' ¹⁵But Jesus answered him, 'Let it be so now; for it is proper for us in this way to fulfil all righteousness.' Then he consented. ¹⁶And when Jesus had been baptised, just as he came up from the water, suddenly the heavens were opened to him and he saw the Spirit of God descending like a dove and alighting on him. ¹⁷And a voice from heaven said, 'This is my Son, the Beloved, with whom I am well pleased.'

## Initial observations

The baptism of Jesus by John is referred to in all four Gospels. 'Referred to' rather than recounted because while Mark tells the story more or less straightforwardly, the other accounts show varying degrees of unease. The origin of the unease is probably two-fold. First of all, the baptism shows Jesus 'submitting' to John and receiving from him. One could conclude that the one who gave was greater than the one who received. In the second place, at the time the Gospels were actually written there were still followers of John the Baptist around. Perhaps part of their identity over against the Christian movement was that John was the mentor and Jesus a disciple of his. One of the side-effects of this unease with John's Baptism of Jesus is that the baptism is one of the most historically certain events in the Gospels, because the early Christians would not have 'developed' an account which gave them so much trouble.

The trouble it did give them becomes apparent in today's excerpt – the conversation shows John realising that something was not quite right in *his* baptising Jesus. This is unlikely to be historical – it is not found in Mark, the vocabulary is Matthean (see below), and it is in tension with the question of the Baptist regarding the identity of Jesus in Matthew 11:2–6. The unease is more marked in Luke, where, from a narrative point of view, John seems to be in prison when the baptism takes place (see Lk 3:18–22)! Again, in John's Gospel, the Baptism is avoided and not recounted (although the associated phenomena are – see Jn 1:29–34).

## Kind of writing

The first scene, with a basis in history, is an anecdote (a *chreia*), telling of a key turning point in the career of Jesus. The Transfiguration will be similarly significant. The second scene, resonant with symbolism, expresses the transcendent meaning of the baptism for Jesus (awareness of Sonship and the gift of the Spirit) and also for the first Christians.

## Old Testament background

### Ritual Washing

Ritual washing is known in the Old Testament and was widely used in Qumran by the community of the Dead Sea Scrolls. John's baptism seems to be different – marking acceptance of his programme rather than ritual purification.

### 'Voice Over the Water'

The 'voice over the water' is an echo of Psalm 29, today's responsorial psalm. The Spirit over the water is an echo of Genesis 1:1–2; 'like a dove' perhaps echoes the story of Noah's flood, with the dove signaling the beginning of the end of the disaster.

### 'This Is My Son'

'This is my Son' may echo the enthronement Psalm 2, used in the New Testament as a messianic text (Acts 4:25–26; 13:33; Heb 1:5; Rev 2:27).

## New Testament foreground

### Transfiguration Accounts

> While he was still speaking, suddenly a bright cloud overshadowed them, and from the cloud a voice said, 'This is my Son, the Beloved; with him I am well pleased; listen to him!' (Mt 17:5 ; Mk 9:7; Lk 9:35)

> For he received honour and glory from God the Father when

that voice was conveyed to him by the Majestic Glory, saying, 'This is my Son, my Beloved, with whom I am well pleased.' (2 Pet 1:17 )

## Righteousness

Matthew, with a strong Jewish identity, has a special interest in 'righteousness', as can be seen from the Gospel occurrences: Mt (7), Mk (0), Lk (1), Jn (2). In our particular setting, righteousness retains its Old Testament meaning of 'to act correctly within a relationship'. In this instance, the right thing for John to do is to baptise Jesus. 'Proper' and 'prevent' are *hapax* in the Gospels. In the Synoptics, 'to fulfil' is a strong Matthew word: Mt (16), Mk (2), Lk (9), Jn (15).

## God's Son

That Jesus is God's Son is made plain in Matthew's Gospel:

But just when he had resolved to do this, an angel of the Lord appeared to him in a dream and said, 'Joseph, son of David, do not be afraid to take Mary as your wife, for the child conceived in her is from the Holy Spirit. She will bear a son, and you are to name him Jesus, for he will save his people from their sins.' (Mt 1:20–21)

'Look, the virgin shall conceive and bear a son, and they shall name him Emmanuel,' which means, 'God is with us.' (Mt 1:23)

The tempter came and said to him, "If you are the Son of God, command these stones to become loaves of bread."' (Mt 4:3)

… saying to him, 'If you are the Son of God, throw yourself down; for it is written, "He will command his angels concerning you," and "On their hands they will bear you up, so that you will not dash your foot against a stone."' (Mt 4:6)

At that time Jesus said, 'I thank you, Father, Lord of heaven and earth, because you have hidden these things from the wise and the intelligent and have revealed them to infants; yes, Father, for such was your gracious will. All things have been handed over to me by my Father; and no one knows the Son except the Father, and no one knows the Father except the Son and anyone to whom the Son chooses to reveal him.' (Mt 11:25–27)

Simon Peter answered, 'You are the Messiah, the Son of the living God.' (Mt 16:16)

Now when the centurion and those with him, who were keeping watch over Jesus, saw the earthquake and what took place, they were terrified and said, 'Truly this man was God's Son!' (Mt 27:54)

## St Paul

As many of you as were baptised into Christ have clothed yourselves with Christ. There is no longer Jew or Greek, there is no longer slave or free, there is no longer male and female; for all of you are one in Christ Jesus. And if you belong to Christ, then you are Abraham's offspring, heirs according to the promise. (Gal 3:27–29)

## Brief commentary

(V. 13)

Jesus came to John from Nazareth, in Galilee. John was a prophet, proclaiming the last days, offering an immersion in water which symbolised the conversion to God's word as revealed to John himself. Jesus was definitely a follower, as is shown by the baptism and also by the timing of the start of Jesus' ministry. Implied in the withdrawal to the desert from Jerusalem is a critique of the temple cult (as can also be seen in Jesus' ministry). Baptise here means basically to 'immerse' and is not to be confused with the later Christian rite.

(V. 14)

This Matthean addition has been accounted for above. This extra Matthean verse communicates the unease of the writer and perhaps his community (in Antioch on the Orontes).

(V. 15)

Each has a role within a relationship, which includes relationship with God. Righteousness is a kind of code word here meaning the right fulfilment of the Scriptures. Thus, John acts 'righteously'.

(V. 16)

Notice that the actual baptism is not recounted but presumed (a kind of *elipsis*). The symbolism indicates an experience of the numinous – heavens opened, God's Spirit descends. Alighting on him make the symbolism very physical. This was probably not Mark's intention when he spoke of 'like a dove'. However, for Matthew the real meaning is not physical but spiritual.

(V. 17)

A profound affirmation of identity. It has often been noted that the descent of the Holy Spirit marks the end of the relative absence of the Holy Spirit. In rabbinic tradition, it was considered that at this time all one could expect was an echo of the voice of God (a *bat qol*, literally a daughter of the voice). Mark has 'you are my Son', a real echo of Psalm 2. Because Matthew has made clear the Sonship of Jesus already (in Mt 1–2), it makes less sense to use 'you', so Matthew changes the wording to 'this is'. The scene becomes, in Matthew's hands, not only a realisation of Sonship, but a revelation of the Son to the world. This incipiently 'Trinitarian' moment anticipates Matthew 28:19.

## Pointers for prayer

a)  The Baptism of Jesus marks a turning point in his life, and the start of his public ministry. Recall moments when your life changed and you moved into a new phase.

b)  The experience was one in which Jesus had a new sense of his own identity. What have been the experiences that have helped shaped your sense of who you are?

c) How have you come to an awareness of being a child of God, beloved by God, and one on whom rests the grace of God?

d) It is surprising that Jesus, the Saviour of the world, asks to be baptised by John. The request symbolises his desire to identify with us. At the same time he is filled with the Holy Spirit. That step of identifying with us is an important element in his being able to help us. Have you ever found that when someone identifies with you, it is easier for him/her to help you? Has your ability to identify with others had any impact on your effectiveness in helping others?

## Prayer

*God of the covenant, you anointed your beloved Son with the power of the Holy Spirit, to be the light of the nations and release for captives.*

*Grant that we who are born again of water and the Spirit may proclaim with our lips the good news of his peace and show forth in our lives the victory of his justice.*

*We make our prayer through Jesus Christ, your Word made flesh, who lives and reigns with you in the unity of the Holy Spirit, in the splendour of eternal light, God for ever and ever. Amen.*

## 🌿 Second Reading 🌿

**Acts 10:34** Then Peter began to speak to them: 'I truly understand that God shows no partiality, *³⁵but in every nation anyone who fears him and does what is right is acceptable to him. ³⁶You know the message he sent to the people of Israel, preaching peace by Jesus Christ – he is Lord of all. ³⁷*That message spread throughout Judea, beginning in Galilee after the baptism that John announced: *³⁸*how God anointed Jesus of Nazareth with the Holy Spirit and with power; how he went about doing good and healing all who were oppressed by the devil, for God was with him. *³⁹ We are witnesses to all that he did both in Judea and in Jerusalem. They put him to death by hanging him on a tree; ⁴⁰but God raised him on the third day and allowed him to appear, ⁴¹not to all the people but to us who were chosen by God as witnesses, and who ate and drank with him after he rose from the dead. ⁴²He commanded us to preach to the people and to testify that he is the one ordained by God as judge of the living and the dead. ⁴³All the prophets testify about him that everyone who believes in him receives forgiveness of sins through his name.'*

## Initial observations

The Acts of the Apostles is offered as history. However, it is not quite history as we would imagine it today. The writer does indeed use sources and tells a story in sequence. However, the overall purpose is persuasion, that is, to bring people to a new understanding of the Gospel for their time (and ours). In particular, there are three dimensions which influence the telling: the role of the Holy Spirit, the ideals of the community and the career of Paul. Within that, the writer offers speeches at significant moments. How much of these go back to the events is a moot point. They seem to reflect a mature biblical appropriation of the Jesus tradition and reflect more or less entirely the language and outlook of the writer. Such 'history' with words put on the lips of characters was completely normal at the time. The long story of Cornelius and his household occupies a pivotal position in the overall narrative and project of Luke and Acts.

## Kind of writing

This is a highly dramatic telling, unfolding in the context in a number of scenes and interlude:

(Acts 9.43)                    Peter a guest at home of Simon

*Scene 1* (Acts 10:1–8)      Cornelius (revelation)
*Scene 2* (Acts 10:9–16)      Peter (revelation)
*Scene 3* (Acts 10:17–23a)    Peter meets the envoys of Cornelius
*Interlude* (Acts 10:23b–27)   Journey of Peter and entourage; meeting of Peter and Cornelius
*Scene 4* (Acts 10:28–48)     Peter and Cornelius in the latter's home in Caesarea
*Scene 5* (Acts 11:1–18)      Peter explains his actions to the community at Jerusalem.

By means of this layout, Luke narrates the story of Cornelius no fewer than three times, without boring the hearers / readers.

Our selection (Vs 34–43) makes up a distinct unit as follows:

*Scene 4b* (Acts 10:34–43)
A: Vs 34b–35, *universalism*; B: Vs 26–38, *Jesus – what he did*; C: V. 39a, *witnesses*.
A\*: V. 43 *universalism*; B\*: Vs 39b–40, *Jesus – what has done to him*; C\*: Vs 41–42, *witnesses*.

## Context in the community

Acts 9:32–11:18: a unit of teaching. There are three stories about Peter: (1) Acts 9:32–35; (2) Acts 9:36–43; (3) Acts 10:1–11:18 = (a) Acts 10:1–19 the events and (b) Acts 11:1–18 the justification of the events.

All three stories take place in Judea (including the administrative capital, Caesarea Maritima).

## Related passages

> While they were talking about this, Jesus himself stood among them and said to them, 'Peace be with you'. They were startled and terrified, and thought that they were seeing a ghost. He said to them, 'Why are you frightened, and why do doubts arise in your hearts? Look at my hands and my feet; see that it is I myself. Touch me and see; for a ghost does not have flesh and bones as you see that I have.' And when he

had said this, he showed them his hands and his feet. While in their joy they were disbelieving and still wondering, he said to them, 'Have you anything here to eat?' They gave him a piece of broiled fish, and he took it and ate in their presence. (Lk 24:36–43)

## Brief commentary

(Vs 34b–35)

The theme of universalism is a key: cf. Testament of Job 4:8; Romans 2:11; Galatians 2:6; Colossians 3:25; Ephesians 6:9; 1 Peter 1:17; James 2:1, 9; 1 Clement 1:3; Barnabas 4:12; Polycarp, To the Philippians 6:1.

(Vs 36–38)

Jesus' activity as prophet, closely following Luke's Gospel.

(V. 39a)

The witnesses to the ministry of Jesus. Being witnesses is central to the mission in Acts.

(Vs 39b–40)

Jesus is rejected (using the language of Galatians, interestingly); the resurrection (i.e. vindication) is the deed of God.

(Vs 41–42)

These are the witnesses to the resurrection of Jesus. Cf. Luke 24:36–43 (above); Acts 1:4.

(V. 43)

Universalism once more, as already implied in the Pentecost speech. Cf. 'Peter said to them, "Repent, and each one of you be baptised in the name of Jesus Christ for the forgiveness of your sins, and you will receive the gift of the Holy Spirit. For the promise is for you and your children, and for all who are far away, as many as the Lord our God will call to himself."' (Acts 2:38–39). Cf. Luke 2:29–32; 3:6; 4:25–27; 24:47; Acts 1:8.

## Pointers for prayer

a) Witnesses: who has been to me an authentic witness and bearer of the Good News? To whom have I been a witness?

b) Showing partiality is a very human trait and it takes conscious choice to act differently. How have I learned to accept people without prejudice?

c) The need for forgiveness is also a regular human phenomenon, sometimes from myself or from others; from time to time we need forgiveness also from God.

## Prayer

*God, creator of everything and everyone, lover of all humanity without partiality or distinction, help us to live according to the good news of Jesus.*

*Help us to break down barriers just as he did. Show us how to reach out to the excluded, in imitation of Christ who was himself excluded in death, your Son, our Lord Jesus Christ, who lives and reigns with you in the unity of the Holy Spirit, God for ever and ever. Amen.*

## ☙ First Reading ☙

Isa 42:1  Here is my servant whom I support,
my chosen one in whom I take pleasure.
I have placed my spirit on him;
he will make just decrees for the nations.

² He will not cry out or shout;
he will not publicise himself in the streets.

³ A crushed reed he will not break,
a dim wick he will not extinguish;
he will faithfully make just decrees.

⁴ He will not grow dim or be crushed
before establishing justice on the earth;
the coastlands will wait in anticipation for his decrees.

5 This is what the true God, the LORD, says–
the one who created the sky and stretched it out,
the one who fashioned the earth and everything that
lives on it,
the one who gives breath to the people on it,
and life to those who live on it:
6 I, the LORD, officially commission you;
I take hold of your hand.
I protect you and make you a covenant mediator for people,
and a light to the nations,
7 to open blind eyes,
to release prisoners from dungeons,
those who live in darkness from prisons.

## Initial Observations

The present text is a kind of calling or appointment oracle. As such, it suits very well because the baptism was for Jesus a moment when his identity and future role became apparent to him.

## Kind of writing

As indicated above, today we read one of the four poems in Second Isaiah, known as the Suffering Servant Songs (Isa 42:1–4; 49:1–6; 50:4–9; 52:13–53:12). It is not entirely clear what these songs may have meant at the time of writing. The somewhat mysterious servant can be singular or plural, it can be in the second person or third person, it can also have a collective or corporate meaning. Ultimately, this polyvalent imagery seems to point to the prophet as an individual called to live the suffering of exile in an exemplary manner to that the people too may know how to live this bitter experience in grace. When the servant is said to suffer 'for' the people, this is not substitutionary ('in place of') but exemplary ('for the benefit of'). In Vs 1–4, the servant is present to the court. In Vs 6–7, the servant himself is addressed directly, following the identification of God as the creator of all in V. 5.

## Origins of the reading

The context is Second Isaiah, the unnamed prophet whose teachings are gathered in Isaiah 40–55. He was active, it would seem, towards the end of Babylonian exile and, when all seemed lost, he raised the spirits of the exiles to place their hope once more in God. Within Second Isaiah, 42:1–7 are found in the longer context 41:21–42:12, in which the Lord (YHWH) is shown defending his choice of Cyrus, his chosen instrument.

## Related readings

The Lord GOD has given me the tongue of a teacher, that I may know how to sustain the weary with a word. Morning by morning he wakens – wakens my ear to listen as those who are taught. The Lord GOD has opened my ear, and I was not rebellious, I did not turn backward. I gave my back to those who struck me, and my cheeks to those who pulled out the beard; I did not hide my face from insult and spitting. The Lord GOD helps me; therefore I have not been disgraced; therefore I have set my face like flint, and I know that I shall not be put to shame; he who vindicates me is near. Who will contend with me? Let us stand up together. Who are my adversaries? Let them confront me. It is the Lord GOD who helps me; who will declare me guilty? All of them will wear out like a garment; the moth will eat them up. (Isa 50:4–9)

## Brief commentary

(V. 1)
The 'policy' of the heavenly court is presented: God will commission a new servant – Cyrus – to carry out his will. The word 'judgment', which occurs three times here, needs to be translated as verdict or judgment arrived at.

(Vs 2–3)

The meaning seems to be that he will not proceed by force or violence. The bruised read and the dimly burning wick must refer to the weakened state of the exiles.

(V. 4)

This new servant will not be discouraged by anything. It is a surprise to find 'his teaching' (literally *torah*) at the end. Of course, the 'his' is ambiguous but really refers to the *torah* of YHWH. At this point, the term had not yet become a technical expression for the Pentateuch. '*Torah*' or teaching is important in Isaiah 1–55 (Isaiah 1:10; 2:3; 5:24; 8:16, 20; 24:5; 30:9; 42:4, 21, 24; 51:4, 7).

(V. 5)

Here the Lord is presented as the creator of the world. The Hebrew reads, 'the El, YHWH'. God's universal control of history is evoked. There is surely an echo of Genesis 1.

(V. 6)

Cyrus is directly addressed and his role described in very high terms. V. 6a describes how God will protect Cyrus, having taken him by the hand. V. 6b describes his double role, as a covenant to Israel and a light to all other nations. The writer does not hesitate to use traditional terms of tremendous religious import to speak of the Persian leader.

(V. 7)

The calling of Cyrus is made very concrete in relation to the exiles: V. 7a restoring sight, V. 7b setting free, V. 7c both terms together, setting free those in darkness.

## Pointers for prayer

a) When have you experienced in your own life that gentleness and non-violence achieve more than force and dominance?

b) The sense of being held by God and kept by him is very powerful in this reading. Can you name such experiences in your own life?

## Prayer

*God, you know us all by name and hold us all by the hand.*
*Grant we pray the gift of faith – absolute trust in you –*
*that we too may know that in you we live and move and have our being.*
*Through Christ our Lord. Amen.*

# Chapter 13

## Second Sunday of Year A

### Thought for the day

In John's Gospel, the first thing that any human being says of Jesus is found on the lips of John the Baptist: 'Look, there is the Lamb of God'. We think naturally and correctly of the Passover lamb and of the Passover, the feast which marks the liberation of Israel. To be set free is a wonderful experience and we could reflect on how I experience my freedom in Christ. *From what* have I been set free? (For example, fear of death, the risk of absurdity, sins and false directions in life … ). Even more important, *for what* have I been set free?

### Prayer

*Jesus, Lamb of God, help me to recognise whatever in me*
*is holding me back from life in abundance:*
*give me your life, your forgiveness, your healing. In you, I put my trust.*

### 🌿 Gospel 🌿

**Jn 1:29** The next day John saw Jesus coming toward him and declared, 'Here is the Lamb of God who takes away the sin of the world! ³⁰This is he of whom I said, 'After me comes a man who ranks ahead of me because he was before me.' ³¹I myself did not know him; but I came baptising with water for this reason, that he might be revealed to Israel. '

³²And John testified, 'I saw the Spirit descending from heaven like a dove, and it remained on him. ³³I myself did not know him, but the one who sent me to baptise with water said to me, 'He on whom you see the Spirit descend and remain is the one who baptises with the Holy Spirit.' ³⁴And I myself have seen and have testified that this is the Son of God.'

## Initial Observations

In the tradition of the liturgical year, there are three 'epiphanies' of Jesus: the first is the feast of the Epiphany (Jan 6), the second is the Baptism of the Lord (the following Sunday) and the third is the Wedding Feast of Cana (the next Sunday). With the current three-year lectionary, the Cana story is read in the year of Luke. For the other two years, an 'epiphany' moment from John's Gospel is used – today it is the witness of the Baptist to Jesus.

It is very often the case in the Fourth Gospel that we are (over)hearing not the historical words of John (or others) but rather the theology, the spiritual teaching of the evangelist and the community of the time of writing.

## Kind of writing

This is quite scenic, even theatrical writing. The author uses considerable freedom to create a narrative which makes John the Baptist identify Jesus and reveal him to Israel. This is unlikely to be historical – witness the questions of the Baptist in Matthew 7:18–20 and parallels. The language used is thoroughly Johannine:

*the next day*: Mt (1), Mk (1), Lk (0), Jn (5)
*lamb*: Mt (0), Mk (0), Lk (0), Jn (2)
*sin*: Mt (6), Mk (7), Lk (11), Jn (17)
*world*: Mt (9), Mk (3), Lk (3), Jn (78)
*this is the one*: Mt (14), Mk (4), Lk (7), Jn (18)
*revealed*: Mt (0), Mk (3), Lk (0), Jn (9)
*witness*: Mt (1), Mk (0), Lk (1), Jn (33)

*remain or abide*: Mt (3), Mk (2), Lk (7), Jn (40)
*know*: Mt (24), Mk (21), Lk (25), Jn (84)
*send*: Mt (4), Mk (1), Lk (10), Jn (32)

This means we are dealing with a text full of Johannine vocabulary and theology. Everything in this Gospel is really centred on Christ and these scenes represent a remarkable theology of the identity of Jesus, the risen Lord present in the community of faith.

*Scenes*

Day 1: scene one, 'who are you?' (Jn 1:19–23); scene two, 'why do you baptise?' (Jn 1:24–28).

Day 2: scene three, 'the purpose of John's baptism' (Jn 1:29–31); scene four, 'the identity of Jesus, baptiser in the Spirit' (Jn 1:32–34).

The opening narrative of the Fourth Gospel is carefully choreographed. The author is keen to relate and, even more, to distinguish the persons and roles of John and Jesus. All four scenes are connected (notice the number of denials by John) and lead to the climactic identification of Jesus. John the Baptist gives the first 'human' reaction to Jesus in the Fourth Gospel and the image used – Lamb of God – is laden with meaning.

## Old Testament Background

The LORD said to Moses and Aaron in the land of Egypt: This month shall mark for you the beginning of months; it shall be the first month of the year for you. Tell the whole congregation of Israel that on the tenth of this month they are to take a lamb for each family, a lamb for each household. If a household is too small for a whole lamb, it shall join its closest neighbour in obtaining one; the lamb shall be divided in proportion to the number of people who eat of it. Your lamb shall be without blemish, a year–old male; you may take it from the sheep or from the goats. You shall keep it until the fourteenth day of this month; then the whole assembled congregation of Israel shall slaughter it at twilight. They shall take some of the blood and put it on the two doorposts and the lintel of the houses in which they eat it. They shall eat the lamb that same night; they shall eat it roasted over the fire with unleavened bread and bitter herbs. (Ex 12:1–8)

## New Testament Foreground

### Jesus as the Lamb of God

The author has several things in view. Firstly, Jesus fulfils the symbolism of the Passover of Lamb, bringing a new liberation by his death. Secondly, Jesus is delivered to death at the moment when the slaughter of the Passover lambs started (Jn 19:14). There is some link with the Good Shepherd language and laying down one's life for the sheep.

### The Pre-existence of the Word

The pre-existence of the Word is already plain from John 1:1–18: 'John testified to him and cried out, "This was he of whom I said, 'He who comes after me ranks ahead of me because he was before me.'"' (Jn 1:15). Later in the Gospel, at the expense of grammar, theology is made clear: 'Jesus said to them, "Very truly, I tell you, before Abraham was, I am"' (Jn 8:58).

### Sender of the Spirit

Jesus is the sender of the Spirit in the Fourth Gospel: John 14:16–17, 26; 15:26; 16:7, 13; 19:30; 20:22.

### 'The One Sent Me'

'The one sent me' is practically a name for God in this Gospel: John 1:33; 4:34; 5:24, 30, 37; 6:38–39, 44; 7:16, 28, 33; 8:16, 18, 26, 29; 9:4; 12:44–45, 49; 13:20; 14:24; 15:21; 16:5. The really pregnant text which combines these themes is: '"As the Father has sent me, so I send you." When he had said this, he breathed on them and said to them, "Receive the Holy Spirit" (Jn 20:21–23).

## St Paul

> Your boasting is not a good thing. Do you not know that a
> little yeast leavens the whole batch of dough? Clean out the
> old yeast so that you may be a new batch, as you really are
> unleavened. For our paschal lamb, Christ, has been sacrificed.
> Therefore, let us celebrate the festival, not with the old yeast,
> the yeast of malice and evil, but with the unleavened bread of
> sincerity and truth. (1 Cor 5:6–8)

## Brief Commentary

(V. 29)

John and Jesus seem not to meet in this Gospel (the baptism as such
is not recounted here). Again, nothing prepares us for the identification
of Jesus with the Lamb of God. It is historically most unlikely that John
the Baptist made such a proclamation, as we have seen. Rather, we have
here the spiritual teaching of the Fourth Gospel, which does indeed
identify Jesus as our Passover Lamb, as is evident in the details of the
death of Jesus in this Gospel: noon, hyssop, not breaking the bones. Noon
was the established time when it was permitted to begin slaughtering
the Passover lambs (Jn 19:14). Hyssop is impractical for sustaining a
sponge, but it echoes the instructions for the Passover (Jn 19:29). The
breaking of the legs is found only in this Gospel; again, it echoes the
instructions for the Passover lamb (Jn 19:33). The human issue of sin
(sin as such, and not sins) will be 'resolved' by Jesus as he discloses the
astonishing love of God both in his teaching and in his 'lifting up'. Cf.
'For God so loved the world that he gave his only Son, so that everyone
who believes in him may not perish but may have eternal life' (Jn 3:16).

(V. 30)

Johannine anxiety about the relatedness and distinction of Jesus and
John comes to the fore here. Once more, this high Christology represents
the teaching not of John the Baptist, of course, but that of the evangelist
and his community. Although it seems historically unquestioned that
John was the older of the two, here 'he (Jesus) was before me'. This takes

us back to the deep origins of Jesus in God, as explored in the Prologue of John. Cf. John 8:58 above.

(V. 31)

Behind the deep theology may be a factual memory of John's genuine ignorance of the person he was sent to introduce. There may also be historical fidelity in the limited revelation to Israel. This Gospel knows that Jesus is the saviour of the world, but John – in fact – had a mission only to Israel. John's baptism is 'only' symbolic; Jesus' baptism will confer the reality, the Holy Spirit.

(V. 32)

In this verse we come as near as this Gospel will allow us to the baptism of Jesus by John, one of the most certain things about the life of the historical Jesus. (See the previous Sunday's notes for an explanation of this reticence.) However, the baptism is actually not recounted, although the accompanying symbols indicating a transcendent experience are indeed present. The witness of John is given first, and only then the chronologically prior revelation from God. Witness is a hugely important term for the Fourth Gospel and here John is shown as the first, truthful witness about Jesus.

(V. 33)

The interpretation, given before to John, is only now recounted, almost as a confirmation before and after the fact. That the Spirit remains/ abides is a key because Jesus will give the Spirit in such a new way that it is almost as if there were no Spirit active before him.

(V. 34)

'Seen and testified' – all pure Johannine language. 'Son of God' is used more frequently of Jesus in this Gospel that in any other, Mt (8), Mk (8), Lk (10), Jn (18). Cf. 'We declare to you what was from the beginning, what we have heard, what we have seen with our eyes, what we have looked at and touched with our hands, concerning the word of life – this life was revealed, and we have seen it and testify to it, and declare to you the eternal life that was with the Father and was revealed to us – we declare to you what we have seen and heard so that you also may have fellowship with us; and truly our fellowship is with the Father and with his Son Jesus Christ. We are writing these things so that our joy may be complete' (1 Jn 1:1–4).

## Pointers for Prayer

a) The words of John point to a deep recognition of Jesus' identity. Can I recall times when this recognition took place for me, first of all on a human level, and then on the faith level?

b) John the Baptist admits to not knowing him – a place of real honesty which is the beginning of the pilgrimage of faith. At some point, perhaps, I heard the words of the Psalmist in my heart: 'a voice I did not know said to me, I freed your shoulder from the burden' (Ps 81).

c) What is my own conviction about being sent and about the one sending me? Prayer of call and response.

d) Jesus baptises with the Spirit – a baptism I too have received, perhaps too young. In later life, there can be an awakening of the Spirit, an inner hunger and thirst, a sense of the Spirit's help in our weakness. Prayer of Romans 8:26–27.

e) Witness is the key. Who have been witnesses to me of the Good News? To whom am I today a witness? Prayer of 1 John 1:1–4.

## Prayer

*Merciful God, you sent your Son, the spotless Lamb,*
*to take upon himself the sin of the world.*

*Make our lives holy, that your Church may bear witness*
*to your purpose of reconciling all things in Christ,*
*who lives and reigns with you in the unity of the Holy Spirit,*
*God for ever and ever. Amen.*

*Soli Deo gloria!*

## 🌿 Second Reading 🌿

**1 Cor 1:1** From Paul, called to be an apostle of *Christ Jesus* by the will of God, and Sosthenes, our brother, 2 to the church of God that is in Corinth, to those who are sanctified in *Christ Jesus*, and called to be saints, with all those in every place who call on the name of our Lord *Jesus Christ*, their Lord and ours. 3 Grace and peace to you from God our Father and the Lord *Jesus Christ*!

### Initial observations

The extensive correspondence with Corinth gives us a unique insight into the community and Paul's relationship with them. Clearly he loved them; just as clearly, they drove him mad! There's a great deal of reconciliation and patching up across 1 and 2 Corinthians.

### Kind of writing

1 Corinthians is a letter, showing the usual features, and at the same time a 'persuasion', following the culturally available categories of Hellenistic rhetoric. We may outline it as follows:

| | |
|---|---|
| 1:1–3 | Epistolary superscript |
| 1:4–9 | Thanksgiving/Introduction |
| 1:10–15:58 | Deliberative argument |
| 16 | Appeal and epistolary conclusion |

We will see the various arguments as the letter is explored over the coming Sunday. For the moment, it is enough to note that our reading is simply opening of the letter and the greeting.

### Context in the community

The Corinthians Christians were experiencing divisions among themselves. This is partly a fruit of there being different house churches and partly the fruit of straightforward disagreement on moral, social, sacramental and doctrinal issues. While the divisions are not along the Jewish/Gentile divide known from Romans and Galatians, they are just as harmful to Paul's overall project, the communion of all humanity in Christ. For the foundation of the Church during Paul's second missionary journey, see Acts 18:

> After this Paul left Athens and went to Corinth. There he found a Jew named Aquila, a native of Pontus, who had recently come from Italy with his wife Priscilla, because Claudius had ordered all Jews to leave Rome. Paul went to see them, and, because he was of the same trade, he stayed with them, and they worked together—by trade they were tentmakers. Every sabbath he would argue in the synagogue and would try to convince Jews and Greeks. (Acts 18:1–4)

Corinth was a very large service city, recently 're-founded' by Julius Caesar. It had a reputation for immorality but was probably no worse than other ports around the Mediterranean. The usual temples and shrines have been found: Apollo, Athena, Poseidon, Hera, Aphrodite, Heracles, Jupiter Capitolinus, Asklepios, Isis and Serapis. There was also at least one synagogue.

## Related passages

The superscripts can be short and long. Longer ones are laden with theology and often anticipate the issues to come. Here are two examples:

> From Paul and Silvanus and Timothy, to the church of the Thessalonians in God the Father and the Lord Jesus Christ. Grace and peace to you! (1 Thess 1:1)

> From Paul, a slave of Christ Jesus, called to be an apostle, set apart for the gospel of God. This gospel he promised beforehand through his prophets in the holy scriptures, concerning his Son who was a descendant of David with reference to the flesh, who was appointed the Son-of-God-

in-power according to the Holy Spirit by the resurrection from the dead, Jesus Christ our Lord. Through him we have received grace and our apostleship to bring about the obedience of faith among all the Gentiles on behalf of his name. You also are among them, called to belong to Jesus Christ. To all those loved by God in Rome, called to be saints: Grace and peace to you from God our Father and the Lord Jesus Christ! (Rom 1:1–7)

## Brief commentary

(V. 1)

Ancient letters began with the name of the sender. Paul gives a careful description of himself: his vocation ('called'), his role ('apostle'), his authority ('will of God'). This is not at all accidental. The Corinthians tended to factionalism and at least some of them had replaced Paul with Apollos in their esteem and affection. Cf. 'For though you may have ten thousand guardians in Christ, you do not have many fathers, because I became your father in Christ Jesus through the gospel' (1Cor 4:15). Paul was not one of the Twelve Apostles but always considered himself their equal. In Acts 18, a certain Sosthenes is mentioned: 'So they all seized Sosthenes, the president of the synagogue, and began to beat him in front of the judgment seat' (Acts 18:17). Like Paul, he was a Jew who became a Christ believer.

(V. 2)

The word 'church' (*ekklesia*) is neutral, meaning an assembly of any kind. Thus, it requires qualification: the assembly *of God in Corinth*. 'Saints' means simply believers and is the ancient equivalent of Christians. Notice that Paul typically combines, even in this simple greeting, his trade-mark of indicative ('are sanctified') and imperative ('called to be saints'). Cf. 'And may the Lord cause you to increase and abound in love for one another and for all, just as we do for you, so that your hearts are strengthened in holiness to be blameless before our God and Father at the coming of our Lord Jesus with all his saints' (1 Thess 3:12–13), 'Some of you once lived this way. But you were washed, you were sanctified, you were justified in the name of the Lord Jesus Christ and by the Spirit of our God' (1 Cor 6:11).

Paul goes on to mention 'all in every place', thereby signally a wider communion, which will be the very challenge as he writes to the Corinthians. However, 1 Corinthians is not a general epistle but is quite specifically focused on the issues emerging in Corinth. See the teaching on the Eucharist (ch. 11) and the teaching on the gifts (ch. 12–14).

(V. 3)

Grace reflects the notion of *unexpected* gift or favour, triggering a sense of gratitude. It also points to the spiritual gifts, a point of contention. Peace or communal harmony is the very thing they lack. Notice no fewer than four mentions of Christ in a very brief passage. 1 Corinthians opens with an intense reflection on the crucifixion of Jesus in chapter 1 and closes with a deep exploration of the resurrection of Jesus in chapter 15.

## Pointers for prayer

a) What is my own sense of being favoured, gifted or graced?

b) What is God asking of me now, so that I may grow in holiness?

## Prayer

*God of every gift and grace, help us to build a community where all are welcome and the gifts of each contribute to the wellbeing of all. Through Christ our Lord. Amen.*

## 🌿 First Reading 🌿

Isa 49:1    Listen to me, O coastlands,
pay attention, you peoples from far away!

> The LORD called me before I was born,
> while I was in my mother's womb he named me.
> <sup>2</sup> He made my mouth like a sharp sword,
> in the shadow of his hand he hid me;
> he made me a polished arrow,
> in his quiver he hid me away.
> <sup>3</sup> And he said to me, 'You are my servant,
> Israel, in whom I will be glorified.'
> <sup>4</sup> But I said, 'I have laboured in vain,
> I have spent my strength for nothing and vanity;
> yet surely my cause is with the LORD,
> and my reward with my God.'

**Isa 49:5**
> And now the LORD says,
> who formed me in the womb to be his servant,
> to bring Jacob back to him,
> and that Israel might be gathered to him,
> for I am honoured in the sight of the LORD,
> and my God has become my strength –
> <sup>6</sup> he says,
> 'It is too light a thing that you should be my servant
> to raise up the tribes of Jacob
> and to restore the survivors of Israel;
> I will give you as a light to the nations,
> that my salvation may reach to the end of the earth.'

## Initial Observations

Following on last Sunday's reading from Isaiah 42 – one of the Suffering Servant Songs – we have today a second song, this time from Isaiah 49. The full song is four verses, 1–4, with a second part in Vs 5–12, sensibly shortened in the Lectionary. The added verses are in italics, as usual.

## Kind of writing

Apart from being poetry, this seems to be a report of the commissioning of the servant. The speaker in Vs 1–4 addresses Israel, reflecting on the call of God. Cf. Isaiah 41:8–10, 43:1–7 and 44:1–5. In some way, the Servant Israel seems not to have accepted the role assigned by God to Cyrus, who is the effective political anointed (messiah) of God. Cf. Isaiah 42:1–4, 44:28–45:7 and 45:13. There is feeling of disappointment in Vs 1–4, in contrast with the energy and confidence in Vs 5–12. Any reader will notice the change of tone in V. 5.

## Origins of the reading

We are in Second Isaiah. For the detailed context, see last week's fairly complete notes on Isaiah and on the songs.

## Related readings

The real context is the other Suffering Servant Songs, that is, Isaiah 42:1–4; 49:1–4; 50:4–9; 52:13–53:12.

> The word of the LORD came to me: Before I formed you in the womb I knew you, before you were born I dedicated you, a prophet to the nations I appointed you. (Jer 1:4–5)

> But when God, who had set me apart before I was born and called me through his grace, was pleased to reveal his Son to me ... (Gal 1:15–16)

## Brief commentary

(V. 1)
Notice the internationality of the address. Coastlands means the Mediterranean seaboard, view from the exile in Babylon. The true prophetic character is called, like Jeremiah earlier, before he was born.

There are important echoes of Genesis 25:23–25 (Jacob and Esau) and Genesis 32:28 (Jacob becomes Israel).

(V. 2)
Notice the military images here: sword, arrow quiver. 2a and 2c go together: a sharp sword and a polished arrow. 2b and 2d go together in terms of protection: shadow of his hand, his quiver. Thus the call is challenging, but YHWH's support affirmed. Israel always thought of itself as having a high role in God's plans.

(V. 3)
Here, Israel is identified as the servant – one of the potential 'candidates' across the songs. To be glorified here means more than to receive honour but rather to be revealed as you. God's 'being' will be made apparent in his liberating action. Cf. 'Remember these things, O Jacob, and Israel, for you are my servant; I formed you, you are my servant; O Israel, you will not be forgotten by me' (Isa 44:21).

(V. 4)
This verse – missing from the reading – captures the moment of failure and disappointment. Even there, we find confidence in God. Israel complains – but without taking responsibility for the exile and without any recognition for the role of Cyrus.

(V. 5)
As before, the 'innocent' expression 'and now' indicates a change of context and perspective: Isaiah 43:1; 44:1; 48:7, 16; 52:5. Vs 5–6 represent a stark contrast with the preceding Vs 1–4. The person now in view is Cyrus or more probably a successor. This time, it is the Lord who is speaking. There is a reprise of V. 1, in an introspective moment. Notice the parallelism (Jacob brought back; Israel gathered) in 5c–d and 5e–f (honoured and Lord; God and strength). As the passage goes on, it seems to refer to someone who is not Israel, but who will help Israel.

(V. 6)
'A light to the nations' takes us well beyond the national and religious issues of Israel. Cf. 'I am the Lord, I have called you in righteousness, I

have taken you by the and and kept you; I have given you as a covenant to the people, a light to the nations' (Isa 42:6).

## Pointers for Prayer

a) A sense of call can reach deeply into our identity, so it is no exaggeration to speak of being call in the womb. Use this image to explore your own sense of vocation as a believer and / or in some special role.

b) A sense of disappointment and bewilderment can be part of our reaction to way things turn out. If this is you at this time, use the feeling of exasperation to explore your own spiritual state right now.

c) Our gifts are not given for our own delight, but for service in the community of faith and even beyond. When has this realisation become a reality for you?

## Prayer

*God, ever loving and always watching over us,*
*help us to recognise you in all that happens us.*
*Help us to respond in the words of the Psalm,*
*here I am, Lord I come to do your will.*

*Soli Deo Gloria!*

# Further reading

This highly selective reading list is offered as a guide for those who will like to take their understanding of the Scripture to another level.

## Books on the Scriptures

Boring, M. Eugene and Fred B. Craddock, *The People's New Testament Commentary*, Louisville KY: Westminster John Knox Press, 2010. The best single volume commentary on the New Testament. Available in hardcover, paperback and for Kindle.

Barton, John, *A History of the Bible. The Books and Its Faiths*. Milton Keynes: Allen Lane, 2019. A truly comprehensive overview of the issues surrounding the writing, reception and interpretation of the Bible.

Dunn, James D. G. and John Rogerson (eds), *Eerdmans Commentary on the Bible*, Grand Rapids (MI): Eerdmans, 2004. A very useful single volume commentary on the whole Bible. Available in hardcover and for Kindle.

## Commentaries on Matthew's Gospel

Boring, M. Eugene, *Matthew* in the New Interpreter's Bible, volume 8. Abingdon: Abingdon Press: 1995, pages 89–509.

Harrington, Daniel, *The Gospel of Matthew*. Sacra Pagina 1; Collegeville (MN): Liturgical Press, 1991.

Luz, Ulrich, *Matthew 1–7 (2007)*, *Matthew 8–20* (2001), *Matthew 21–28* (2005). Hermeneia series. Minneapolis, MN: Augsburg Press, 2001, 2005, 2007. A comprehensive academic commentary on Matthew's Gospel, in three volumes, translated from the original German.

Luz, Ulrich, *The Theology of Matthew*, Cambridge: Cambridge University Press, 1995.

O'Leary, Anne M., *Matthew's Judaization of Mark*, London: T&T Clark, 2006.

Pagola, José, *The Way Opened Up By Jesus. A Commentary on the Gospel of Matthew*, Miami (FL): Convivium Press, 2012.

Stanton, G. N., *A Gospel for a New People. Studies in Matthew*. Edinburgh: Clark, 1992.

Talbert, Charles, *Matthew*, Paideia Commentaries on the New Testament. Ada (MI): Baker Academic, 2010. The Paideia series specialises in the cultural background to the text.

# Biblical Index

The index follows the order of Old Testament books as found in Catholic bibles;
the chapter and verse numbering follows the NRSV.

Matthew